D1387775

THE LONGEST ROAD

AN IRISH PAN-AMERICAN CYCLING ADVENTURE

Ben Cunningham, from County Kildare, became interested in adventure sports and expeditions in his teens. While a student in Trinity College Dublin he spent summer holidays travelling in Australia, Southeast Asia and Europe. Since March 2009 he has qualified as a barrister and is currently in practice. Recent cycling trips have included France, Spain and Norway.

For more information about the author, visit:
www.thelongestroad.ie

To my parents, Carol and Peter

Day 78   Ben cycles on the open road in Baja, Mexico.

THE LONGEST ROAD

AN IRISH PAN-AMERICAN CYCLING ADVENTURE

The Collins Press

FIRST PUBLISHED IN 2013 BY
The Collins Press
West Link Park
Doughcloyne
Wilton
Cork

ISBN: 978-1848891739

Typesetting by Patricia Hope, Dublin
Typeset in Sabon
Printed in Denmark by Nørhaven

CONTENTS

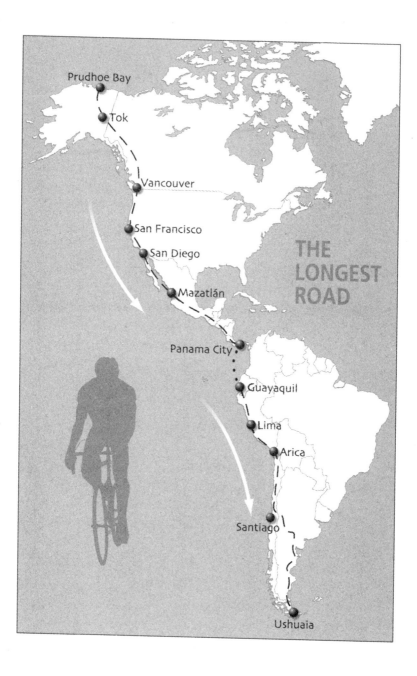

THE
LONGEST
ROAD

Prudhoe Bay
Tok
Vancouver
San Francisco
San Diego
Mazatlán
Panama City
Guayaquil
Lima
Arica
Santiago
Ushuaia

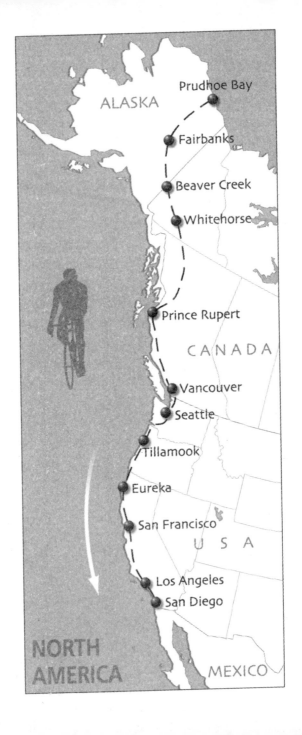

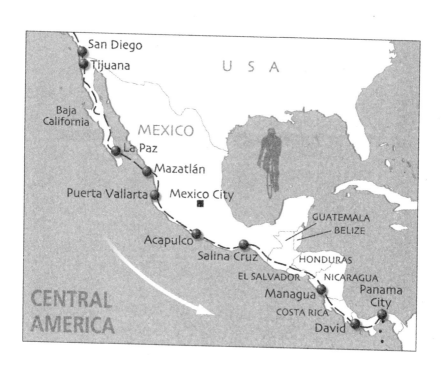

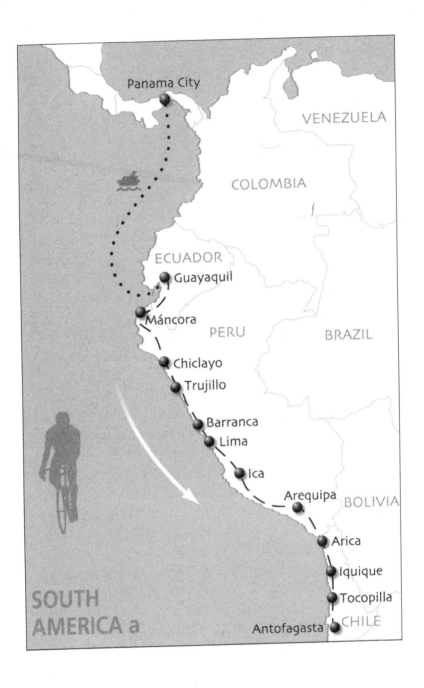

Ica
Arequipa
BOLIVIA
BRAZIL
Arica
Iquique
PARAGUAY
Tocopilla
Antofagasta
Copiapó
ARGENTINA
La Serena
Mendoza
URUGUAY
Santiago
Santa Rosa
CHILE
Trelew
Comodoro Rivadavia
SOUTH
AMERICA b
Ushuaia

INTRODUCTION

In June 2008, five friends and I set out from Prudhoe Bay, Alaska, to cycle to Ushuaia, Argentina. The average age of the cyclists was twenty-two. In Ireland, the expedition generated national interest. It was the first time that a cycling challenge of this length and duration had been attempted by Irish people. This is the story of this compelling adventure.

The Pan-American Highway is believed to be the longest continuous land route in the world. It measures 25,000 km and passes through fourteen different countries and two continents. The Pan-American Highway begins in the northernmost point of Alaska, in a town called Deadhorse, the home of Alaskan oil, and finishes in Ushuaia in Argentina, the world's most southerly city. The road runs through the vast expanses of Alaska and northern Canada and the densely populated cities of Los Angeles and Lima. It moves from hot to cold, from forest to desert, English to Spanish and everything in between.

At the post office in Deadhorse, Alaska, those who started the journey in southern Argentina and completed the route in this barren northern finishing point have pinned to the wall signed Polaroid pictures of themselves along with details of where they're from and how long their journey took. They come from all parts of the world. The times taken to complete the Pan-American Highway vary between the world-record time of four months to the more leisurely pace of two years. On completion, regardless of time, it seems they had all entered into the unofficial fraternity of the Pan-American Highway.

Our aim was to complete the distance in slightly under nine months. This is my story of cycling down the longest road in the world.

Ben Cunningham
County Kildare

PARTICIPANTS IN THE IRISH PAN-AMERICAN CYCLING ADVENTURE

Alan Gray:
Deadhorse (Alaska) to Ushuaia (Argentina)
Kevin Hillier:
Deadhorse (Alaska) to Ushuaia (Argentina)
Brian McDermott:
Deadhorse (Alaska) to Ushuaia (Argentina)
Ben Cunningham:
Deadhorse (Alaska) to Ushuaia (Argentina)
Cillian O'Shea:
Deadhorse (Alaska) to Ushuaia (Argentina)
John Garry:
Deadhorse (Alaska) to Ushuaia (Argentina)
Pat Anglim:
Fairbanks (Alaska) to San Francisco (USA)
Eric Flanagan:
Vancouver (Canada) to San Francisco (USA)
Mike Stewart:
Vancouver (Canada) to San Francisco (USA)
Anthony Quinn:
Vancouver (Canada) to Ensenada (Mexico)
Tom Greaves:
Vancouver (Canada) to Ensenada (Mexico)
Killian Stafford:
Everett (USA) to San Francisco (USA)
Bryan Johnston:
Everett (USA) to San Francisco (USA)
Rob Greene:
San Diego (USA) to Ushuaia (Argentina)

Timi Oyewo:
    Puerto Escondido (Mexico) to Panama City (Panama)

Ben Leonard Kane:
    Arequipa (Peru) to Ushuaia (Argentina)

Chris Wallace:
    Las Grutas (Argentina) to Ushuaia (Argentina)

Paddy O'Connor:
    Playa Bonita (Peru) to Los Andes (Chile)

Conor Shaw:
    Playa Bonita (Peru) to Los Andes (Chile)

Jim Lyons:
    Tacna (Peru) to Ushuaia (Argentina)

Paul Drysdale:
    Tacna (Peru) to Ushuaia (Argentina)

Mark Gray:
    Mendoza (Argentina) to Las Grutas (Argentina)

Support Cycle Mix

Neil 'Stilo' McDermott:
    Deadhorse (Alaska) to Ushuaia (Argentina)

Richard Boyd:
    San Jose, California (USA) to Oxaca (Mexico)

Paul Cahill:
    Insurgantes, Baja (Mexico) to Oxaca (Mexico)

Andrew Wade:
    Insurgantes, Baja (Mexico) to Oxaca (Mexico)

Jenny Doran:
    Insurgantes, Baja (Mexico) to Oxaca (Mexico)

Shauna Lenfesty:
    Barranca (Peru) to Mendoza (Argentina) and
    Las Grutas (Argentina) to Ushuaia (Argentina)

PROLOGUE

21 February 2009

Comodoro Rivadavia, Patagonia, Argentina

Number of days on the road: **247**

Number of kilometres completed: **19,687**

The others are in the sitting room of the rented apartment, chatting. I look at my watch: 6 p.m. and it's getting dark outside.

Suddenly there are three loud bangs on the door downstairs. More loud bangs. I run down and open the door. Two pump-action shotguns are pointing at my chest. Four policemen start screaming at me. I can just about make out what they're saying. One of them shouts, 'You have ten minutes to come up with 4,000 pesos.'

I run back up the stairs, the police behind me. I sense their guns. I'm stuttering and panicking.

'Everyone go to the bank and withdraw your maximum daily amount!' I shout.

The police are yelling at everyone as we run around, gathering all the gear and bussing it downstairs to the street. There's so much stuff to move, so many bikes and parts. Eventually we clear the apartment and get all our belongings outside.

The owner of the building emerges. He's got slicked back greasy hair and he's wearing a shirt opened down to his naval. He's laughing and joking with the men.

We get it all together. Four thousand pesos is a lot of money here. I count it out to the owner in English while he repeats the numbers back to me in Spanish. The police are looking on and laughing. One of them checks the breach of his gun. Suddenly it's over. The police get back into their car and disappear. The owner goes back inside. We remain standing outside, looking at each other, wondering what we've done to deserve this. I look at our gear and bikes scattered around on the side of the road, and then I look up at the stars.

For my part, I travel not to go anywhere, but to go. I travel for travel's sake. The great affair is to move.

ROBERT LOUIS STEVENSON

ALASKA

20 June 2008

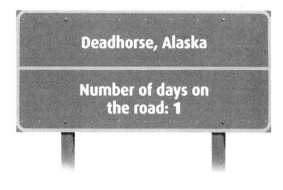

Number of kilometres completed: **2**

I love Alaska already. Thick green Alpine forest rolls across the hills of the horizon as if forever and deep blue skies give everything a crisp definition. Alaska is referred to as the last frontier because of its rugged landscape, its harsh climate and its distance from the rest of the United States. One immediately feels Alaska's intimidating size. It's by far the biggest state in America; an area more than twice that of Texas. If it were a country it would be the nineteenth biggest in the world, a whopping 1,518,800 square kilometres, a vast, almost endless, area of mountains and trees.

We arrive into Deadhorse on the day we're scheduled to start cycling. We've reached the home of Alaskan oil. Commercial oil exploration started here in the 1960s and the main field was discovered on 12 March 1968 by Atlantic Richfield Company or ARCO. In order to service this new oil field, a rough gravel-surfaced road was ploughed straight up through the mountains from Fairbanks to Deadhorse. Consisting of shifting gravel and severe inclines that have become part of travelling lore, the road is known as the Dalton Highway. The oil field itself measures about 24 km by 32. It's the biggest in North America and is operated by British Petroleum. Prudhoe Bay and the auxiliary oil fields that surround it produce one million barrels of oil a day.

Deadhorse is desolate and dreary, an expanse of prefabricated buildings and steel in the featureless tundra. Occasionally we see a caribou or an elk wandering around in the shadow of one of the enormous steel oil structures that dominate the town's periphery.

We're keen to get going as quickly as possible. We nip to the post office to send a few postcards home. I keep a spare one with me that I want to take to the end of the road and post from there. I pin up a photo of our group with today's date alongside the photos of all the other expeditions that have either started or ended here. There are photos of Americans, Spaniards and Japanese, all dated and signed. Most of the groups cycled the distance, some actually walked and there's even a guy who made it here, from where it's not quite clear, on a unicycle.

We drive up to the gate of the oil fields where we're stopped by a security guard. The roads within the oil field area, which lead to the Arctic Ocean, are sealed off and can be accessed only on expensive organised trips. An enormous black man sitting in a small hut beside the gate drawls, 'Y'all can't go any further.'   •

We unload the trailer and begin to put our bikes together. Frames, wheels, tyres, spare parts and all our camping equipment are carefully laid out on the ground. I haven't a clue how to assemble a bicycle and rely on the other lads for assistance. This is my first bike. I've never cycled more than 100 km before.

There are six of us: Alan, Kevin, Brian, myself, Cillian and John. Neil is our support jeep driver and we stayed with him and his girlfriend Cassandra when we flew into Boston eleven days ago. Neil is Brian's brother: he works in Boston as a chef but has put his job on hold to do this trip. A tall, friendly character, he has a laid-back attitude to life and never gets flustered about anything. He is the perfect man to organise the non-cycling aspect of the trip.

It won't matter what time of the day we leave because the sun never goes down here in June – it just moves around the horizon. North of the Arctic Circle the sun can be above or below the horizon for twenty-four continuous hours at least once a year, occurring at the June and December solstices respectively. Tomorrow is the June solstice.

We've been thinking about the starting point for months. We're all quite nervous and the nervousness turns into continuous laughter. Being here and the thought of what's in store is both terrifying and hilarious. John covers himself in Irish tricolours and runs around in a circle. Passing truckers honk their horns.

Just as we finish putting the bikes together, Neil gets a phone call and hears some bad news from Boston: Cassandra has been diagnosed with breast cancer. The laughing stops and easy smiles are replaced with looks of concern. The trip doesn't seem so important now. The only question on our minds is how Neil is going to get back to Boston to be with Cassandra. There's no public transport from Deadhorse to Fairbanks. Flights are expensive and irregular. I begin to feel very isolated. We couldn't be any farther away from anywhere.

Alan and Brian come up to me and suggest that Neil should drive back to Fairbanks alone, leave the jeep at the airport and get the first flight to Boston. We'll make our own way down the Dalton Highway to Fairbanks, with our gear and provisions in panniers. This is a tough decision because, if ever we needed Neil and the support vehicle it's going to be up here during our first days on the Dalton Highway. The mood changes as everyone ponders the development of the past hour and Alan senses this.

'This isn't insurmountable, lads,' he says. 'This is the type of problem we're prepared for.'

Alan came up with the idea for this trip in the first place. He's been a friend of mine since we were small kids growing up in County Kildare. He has put an enormous amount of energy and organisation into planning this expedition so a problem like this won't stop him from starting on time. This isn't a problem; it's an opportunity to place ourselves even further outside our comfort zone. It's a fantastic act of leadership and the intensity and commitment is suddenly electric. Everyone wants to be here. There's not a word of doubt or dissent from anyone. We'll be taking on the Dalton Highway alone without Neil.

Neil rings home to let his family know what's going on. Word of what's happened spreads quickly. Within ten minutes my mother rings Neil's phone. She asks what's happening. I say everything's fine but that Neil's girlfriend has breast cancer and so he's going ahead of us and leaving us on our own for a while. We'll be out of contact in the middle of northern Alaska for the next week, I say. I can hear a sharp intake of breath on the other end of the line.

We have only one mobile phone between us, Neil's, and now he's going back to Boston. Because it's so late, we decide to cycle away from Deadhorse and set up camp a mile farther down the road. Officially, we have begun: one mile, one-point-six kilometres on our first day.

It's 3 a.m. I lie in the tent, which is completely illuminated by the sun. I can't sleep. I wonder how the six of us are going to make it down this road.

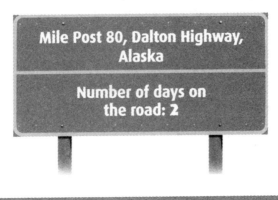

Number of kilometres completed: **132**

Today is the summer solstice. In no other place on earth is today as long; it feels special to be here. Perhaps it's fitting that we start out on the longest road in the world on the longest day of the year.

I think about what I'm doing here and if I'll ever see the end of this road. The challenge seems tougher and more ambitious now than ever before but the mood in the group is upbeat.

'Do you ever think you'll find yourself in Deadhorse again?' I ask Cillian as we clear the town limits. I met Cillian for the first time only a few days ago when we collected himself and John at the airport in Fairbanks. At twenty-four, he's the oldest member of the group; John, who's twenty-one, is the youngest. The two lads are on summer holidays and plan to be with the group until the end of August.

Nothing's taken too seriously with them around; exactly the attitude we need at the moment.

'Not a hope in hell I'll be here again,' Cillian says.

Neil set out in the jeep this morning and we don't know when we'll see him again. On his way back down the road he dropped off water at 128-km intervals. We've packed three smaller back-up tents, six sleeping bags, a camping cooker, camping fuel, two pots, bowls, mosquito head nets, our own spare cycling clothes, a spare tyre, a camera and all the food we need for the three days until we get to Coldfoot, 400 km south. These provisions are packed into panniers and attached to our bikes on either side of the rear wheels.

We're cycling in the North Slope, an area of tundra. The Dalton Highway is often referred to as the North Slope Haul Road. It's flat for the first 160 km and entirely covered in permafrost, a condition where the first 2 feet of the soil's surface remains in a permanently frozen state. The permafrost, combined with the flatness of the land, results in an abundance of small lakes and ponds since melted snow water cannot permeate the hard, frozen ground. The road is flat, varying between poor and bad surfaces. We aim to do 130 km a day. If we do this, we'll get 800 km a week done, including a rest day. This target was set down months ago.

Just off the road, at Mile Post 80 (while in America all signpost distances are in miles, though we think of distances in kilometres), we come upon a wide, open, flat space with a number of prefabricated containers. There is no fence or barrier surrounding the containers. Behind the settlement a stream winds its way back towards the north. It's the first sign of habitation we've seen all day.

I cycle in and have a wander around but there doesn't seem to be anyone here. Behind the main prefab I find a large water tank and fill my water bottle. The group follows me in. The flat cleared ground is ideal for pitching tents and there's water for washing, cooking and drinking. It's the perfect place to stop for the night.

As we start to unload our gear, a woman comes out from one of the containers. She doesn't say anything but looks amazed as she walks towards us, as though she hasn't seen anyone in years. She peers at me through narrowed eyes.

'Sorry for taking your water. I wasn't sure if anyone lived here or not,' I say. 'We're on our way to Argentina.'

'You're a long way from home,' she says, smiling.

She invites us in for dinner and then suggests that, rather than camp out, we can stay in one of her containers. The place we've stumbled upon is a geographical survey base. Geographers, scientists and geologists use this location as their base to access even more remote parts of the state by helicopter. We park our bikes, change out of our cycling gear and have a shower in a container that's been converted into a shower room.

Our hostess is called Luanne and her husband's name is Ed. He tells us he is a native of an even more remote Alaskan settlement called Kaktovik, in the extreme north of the state. Kaktovik was an early-warning centre, used during the Cold War, and is accessible only by plane.

I keep forgetting we're so close to Russia. Much farther to the west, the two countries are divided by the Bering Sea and are only 90 km apart at the sea's narrowest point. The United States purchased Alaska from the Russian Empire for five cents a hectare in 1869, a total of $7.2 million that

Day 3 We line up for a photo with Ed at Mile Post 80 on the Dalton Highway, Alaska, *(l–r):* Ed, Ben, Brian McDermott, Alan Gray, Kevin Hillier, Cillian O'Shea and John Garry.

was viewed by many at the time as being outrageously expensive.

When we arrive for dinner, both Ed and Luanne are quite drunk. Over a meal of beef stroganoff, as he sips a large Scotch, Ed tells us about this region. The area we're in is called Happy Valley because it's where a brothel was situated during the construction of the Dalton Highway. We ask Ed about the huge pipeline that we can see from the road most of the time. He says that since the Arctic Ocean in Prudhoe Bay is ice-free for only six months of the year, the pipe, called the Trans-Alaskan Pipeline, moves North Slope oil from Pump Station Number One in Prudhoe Bay to the ice-free port terminal at Valdez, near Anchorage, 1,300 km to the south. It's an enormous artery of oil which dissects the state. The oil is then transferred by super tankers to refineries on the west coast of the US or the 'lower 48' as Ed puts it, pouring himself another drink. Alaskans refer to the rest of the country, excluding Hawaii, as 'the lower 48'.

We leave Luanne and Ed for the night and go back to our container.

22 June 2008

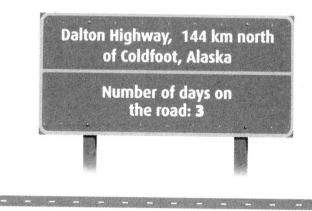

Dalton Highway, 144 km north of Coldfoot, Alaska

Number of days on the road: 3

Number of kilometres completed: **262**

At 10 a.m. Ed is already running about, jabbering into a satellite phone and not showing the faintest trace of a hangover. He gets out his own bike, an old, banged-up racer, so that Luanne can have a photo of us all. After shaking hands with Ed, giving Luanne a hug and all swearing we'll be in touch, we make our way back on to the road. They call after us, 'You boys look after yourselves.'

The road has become less flat and eventually we start to climb and get on to the gravelly surfaces that are more synonymous with the Dalton. This is more like the road we expected. The Dalton Highway, named after its engineer, James Dalton, was built in 170 days in 1974. It gouges through the harsh northern Alaskan environment en route to Fairbanks.

Suddenly we find ourselves in the middle of a

thunderstorm. We're all carrying more then 15 kilos in our panniers. It's hard to keep to a good rhythm. A couple of times my front wheel veers over and slips on the loose, wet gravel on the side of the road and I fall off. It's only the second day and already I'm falling off the bike and picking up some nasty bruises.

At about 3 p.m. we stop for a break at the side of the road and a young Canadian called Mike, who is driving back from Deadhorse to Fairbanks in a pick-up, pulls over. Mike is up here doing some kayaking and hiking. He gives us all his water and I can see he thinks we're going to need it. We're already suffering from fatigue and are beginning to string out along the road.

We take off again and soon a gap of about a hundred metres opens up between us. There's a huge variation in fitness. Some have already done a lot of cycling but John, Cillian and myself have done no worthwhile training and are really struggling. The other three have much more experience. We all persevere at our own pace, grinding out the kilometres. Everyone is far more tired than yesterday and we're getting a feel for how tough this road is. Tomorrow we'll cycle into Brooks Range, a high mountain crossing; we're starting to meet the foothills already. I can see the mountains in the distance, snow-capped and glowing in deep reds and oranges.

On the south side of a small river about 260 km south of Deadhorse, just before the road starts to rise sharply, we set up camp. This requires careful planning. A river or lake means we can drink but, because of the high concentration of grizzly bears, we have been advised to camp at least 2 km upwind from where we eat.

Bears, having hibernated all winter, get very hungry at

this time of year and can smell food from miles away. We haven't seen any bears on the road yet and so we wonder if the warnings were exaggerated and if the bears, if they do exist, will pose any threat.

By the time we set up the tents and begin to prepare the food, we're exhausted. When we finish eating, we leave the cooking utensils and food on one side of the river and camp just over the bridge on the other side, 100 metres away. No one fancies cycling another mile upwind from where we are.

But it turns out the real problem is not bears but mosquitoes. We're not just being bitten occasionally, we're being assaulted by a constant barrage of these moth-sized predators. They pierce our clothes and face netting. Soon our bodies are covered in severe, bloody and lumpy wounds. The only relief is to stand in a stiff breeze or in the smoke from the camp fire. Creams and repellents don't work.

23 June 2008

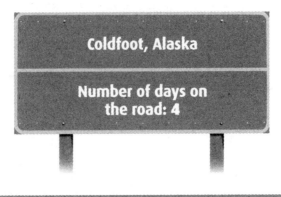

Coldfoot, Alaska

Number of days on
the road: 4

Number of kilometres completed: **404**

We cross the river to get breakfast and see paw marks all over the area where we left the gear. The cooker itself has been overturned. I now recall the loud breathing of an animal last night. I was sharing a tent with Brian but he, jokingly, said it was probably just one of the lads. It scares us. We should have taken more precautions. The only protection we have in the event of an attack is bear spray, a kind of industrial-strength mace. A woman we met in Canada on the way up here told us to get it. She said a girl had been 'ripped limb from limb' while hiking in northern British Columbia a few weeks before. The girl didn't have any bear spray, the woman said.

We pack up and get back on our bikes, all a bit shocked, but we soon forget about it because we're readying ourselves for a tough day. The Atigun Pass, Gobbler's Knob and

Beaver Slide, all difficult climbs, lie between us and the end of the week.

Coming off the tundra and into Brookes Range, we begin to climb towards Atigun Pass, a steep mountain crossing about 3 km long. We can see the crossing in the distance and it looks incredibly steep on the approach. I hear the loud drone of a truck's engine as it weaves down the pass on its way towards us. Atigun, the only road crossing over Brookes Range, has seen many vehicles go off the road and is beset by avalanches during the winter.

Each of us takes on the climb at his own pace. I put the bike in its lowest gear and focus on reaching immediate targets. Though difficult, the pass turns out to be more manageable than we had feared. At the top, we get off the bikes, sit down and catch our breath. Brian takes out a packet of cigarettes and offers them around. We're all smoking at breaks during the day: they have become like small rewards. It wasn't that bad, we all agree; it looked a lot more difficult than it was. From the height we're at, 1,400 metres, there's an amazing view looking back down to the tundra and the North Slope. Through perfectly clear light, we can see the extent of how incredibly flat it has been for the past 320 km. We can see the road weaving down the mountain and back to the horizon until it disappears.

On the other side of the Atigun Pass, my energy drains rapidly and I simply empty out. It's the first time I've ever cycled on four successive days. I was the last person to join this group and I've done almost no training worth talking about; I just didn't have the time before we left home. My neck, elbows and back ache. My head throbs. It has been nine hours since we ate. I fall behind the rest of the group and Kevin drops back to help me along.

Kevin is a strong cyclist. A tall broad guy, he has a lot of natural fitness. He and Alan started organising this trip eighteen months ago and he's had a good deal of practice. Kev and Alan were in school together and studied business in Trinity College. Born and raised in Kenya, Kevin, through his mother's nationality, holds a Dutch passport but has been in Ireland for the past ten years.

I'm running on empty and I tell Kev I can't go on. He cycles ahead and stops the rest of the group who have reached the bank of a small river. When I arrive there I get off the bike and lie down on the riverbank. I'm barely able to speak and I see no one else is doing much talking either. Negative thoughts and huge doubts are filling my mind. I don't know if I'm cut out for this. What was I thinking, taking on such an enormous trip without any cycling experience? I'm struggling badly, disorientated and nauseated. All I want to do is curl up and go to sleep. Lying by the river with my feet dangling in the icy water I wonder how I'm going to stand up, never mind complete the next 48 km to Coldfoot. Alan whips up a highly concentrated energy 'goo' for me; basically a mixture of sugar and caffeine. I choke it down.

Half an hour later I pick myself up and cycle on ten minutes ahead of everyone else. I'm sure it won't be long until I fall behind again or have to stop. But after twenty minutes on the bike I feel surprisingly comfortable. Brian catches up and we cycle together at a strong pace. I eventually go ahead of Brian and pick up the pace even further. I can't believe my progress! I just keep on going. I get into Coldfoot in slightly under two hours. I sing and punch the air from about 5 km out. The bounce back gives me confidence for the days ahead. I sit out on the deck of the town's only restaurant, sip a beer and wait for the rest of the lads to arrive.

Coldfoot is a trucker's stop-off point between Fairbanks and Deadhorse. It consists of a restaurant, a petrol station, a hotel and an airstrip. The settlement was originally a mining camp called Slate Creek but got its present name in 1900 when gold prospectors going up the nearby Koyukuk River would get 'cold feet' here and turn back.

By the time the group arrives everyone is exhausted, hungry, dirty and covered in mosquito bites. Coldfoot's restaurant is mainly for truckers but there are some bikers and a few other tourists too. Truckers love the Dalton, especially in winter when it's constantly dark and the road is covered in ice: dangerous but a true test of a driver, they say. I speak to one of them, who regards it as one of the toughest tests in trucking. He says there's even a television show called *Ice Truckers*, which has documented the drivers travelling up and down the Dalton Highway during winter.

This is an expensive place. Instead of staying at the hotel, which costs $100 a night each, we camp on a grassy area behind it, which is free. Brian and I are nervous as our college exam results are out today. We were doing our final exams in Trinity College right up to when we left Ireland. I've spent the past four years doing a degree in history and economics; Brian has been studying economics and geography. We were so excited about the trip at the time that the exams didn't seem like a big deal. I don't even know if I'm excited about them now. Brian rings home and finds out his results – they're good! – but I decide to wait until Fairbanks. The results don't matter so much when compared with the next three days of cycling down this highway.

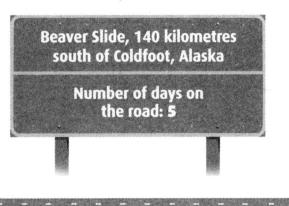

Beaver Slide, 140 kilometres
south of Coldfoot, Alaska

Number of days on
the road: 5

Number of kilometres completed: **512**

We leave Coldfoot at about 12.30 p.m. We're still on a very late clock. After a brief flat stretch, we cycle up over Gobbler's Knob, another mountain crossing. At the top of Gobbler's Knob we're about 1,000 metres above sea level. John's reading *The Road to Gobbler's Knob* by Geoff Hill, a guy who rode a motorcycle from Chile up to here. We're at Hill's final destination, cycling back down the route he came up. Maybe motorbikes would have been a better idea than bicycles.

A couple of kilometres on the other side of Gobbler's Knob, after a big decline, we see two cyclists in the distance coming against us. They're both Dutch. One of them, Cornelius, is over sixty. He's cycling a bike that he tells me is twenty years old and has been around the world three times. He's wearing a cotton shirt; his gear is stored in a gym bag that's fastened to the back of his bike with a leather belt and he's wearing a normal pair of sneakers. We wear special cycling shoes that clip directly on to the pedals, our gear is stored in panniers and we're all wearing state-of-the-art cycle-wear.

Cornelius tells me that he cycled up the Dalton thirty years ago, before they started grading the gravel. The two men have just got on their bikes after kayaking down the Yukon River. I offer Cornelius a piece of dried fruit and he chews on an apricot as he tells me about the trip down the Yukon and other tours he's been on: Mexico, South America and Asia. Cornelius says he hopes we make it to the end of our journey. I realise he's saying this from experience because he knows there is a real chance we may not.

We exchange information about the road we've encountered, what the surface is like, where the next services are and whether or not there are many hills on the way. We wish the two men luck and cycle on.

A few kilometres later we stop at a lay-by where a plaque fixed to a massive boulder indicates that we've just left the Arctic Circle, the parallel of latitude that runs approximately 66 degrees north of the equator.

The day saves the toughest challenge until last, a hill Cornelius spoke about. Cillian turns around and points at an enormous grey slope in the distance. It's Beaver Slide, a 1 km long, steeply ascending gravel road with no turns. I get into my lowest gear possible, but it's still difficult to gain any momentum because the surface is loose underneath and the wheels constantly slip. The fact that the climb is completely straight makes it even more mentally challenging than normal. There are no obvious points to aim for along the way to the top. The gradient is in excess of thirty degrees and so the road itself is in our faces the whole way up. It's 11 p.m. and too late in the day for trucks in either direction. A couple of hundred yards from the summit I dismount, exhausted. We all reach the top eventually, get off the bikes and take a look back down Beaver Slide.

As I catch my breath, I reason to myself that conditions are unlikely to be as physically demanding as this as the journey goes on. 'Just keep on going, we're over the worst of it' is something I say to myself constantly. We say this to each other as well. We encourage each other because different people struggle at different times.

We camp on the other side of Beaver Slide, beside a river with a strong flow, where we can wash and get water for drinking and cooking. The mosquitoes are particularly bad. My back, legs and ankles are covered in horribly swollen bites. There's no comfort at all on the Dalton Highway, on or off the bike. Energy within the group is low.

25 June 2008

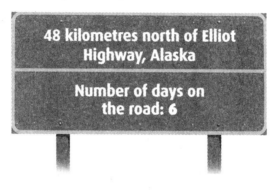

48 kilometres north of Elliot
Highway, Alaska

Number of days on
the road: 6

Number of kilometres completed: **608**

Mosquitoes found their way into my tent last night – I could hear their high-pitched buzzing. I'm delighted to start again this morning and get another day closer to Fairbanks. The breeze on the bikes keeps the mosquitoes at bay. Time spent off the bike is time spent getting bitten.

Sixty-five kilometres down the road we stop at the Hot Spot Café. We're only a few kilometres north of the bridge over the Yukon. At the café, we decide to split up temporarily. Brian and Alan, the strongest cyclists of the group, cycle on ahead to Fairbanks, leaving the rest of us behind. We tuck into the food and soft drinks at the Hot Spot. It's heaven after the rough camping and the tinned tuna of the past few days. The café is run by two fat, middle-aged women. One of them cooks the burgers while the other sits down in the restaurant, analysing and talking to the customers.

'I bet you're the one that keeps the journal,' she says to me, in a way that suggests we're not as original as we think.

She stares at us and chain-smokes while we eat. For the first time in days we all laugh out loud. We chat to these women about politics and again about oil, about Barack Obama and Sarah Palin, the governor of Alaska. Neither of them likes Obama, mainly because he's a Democrat, but also because of his name. They don't think he's really American, they say.

'This guy Barack Hussein Obama thinks he can change the world,' booms the one who is preparing the food. 'Let me tell you something: this is America and America will never change.'

Like Governor Palin, the two women are in favour of drilling for oil in the Arctic National Wildlife Refuge (ANWR), an area of 19 million acres in the northeast of the state which has been set aside for conservation since the 1950s. The North Slope, from where we've just cycled, borders ANWR on its eastern side.

Whether or not to drill in this location has long been an Alaskan and a national debate but congressional authorisation has not yet been granted. More domestic production will result in a reduced dependence on national oil imports but ANWR is an important breeding ground and habitat for dozens of wildlife species such as snow geese and musk oxen. ANWR first became a federally protected area in 1960 but oil was discovered in Alaska in 1968. The topic has been used by Democrats and Republicans as a political tool ever since; to drill or not to drill. Generally, the Republicans favour drilling while the Democrats don't. Since Alaska received official statehood in 1959, every single

Governor to represent the state has been in favour of drilling in ANWR. Sarah Palin has not bucked that trend.

After lunch we cycle down the river valley and eventually come to the E.L Patton Yukon River Bridge. The river is wide at this point and has a fantastic backdrop of thick green forestry on either side. We cross the bridge and climb up the valley on the other side. As we climb higher, I look back and see the sun shining brightly on the river behind us, as it meanders through the hills and thick forestry for kilometres into the distance. Our reduced group camps in a truck lay-by 24 km south of the river at the top of a long climb. We leave ourselves a huge downhill for tomorrow. We're only a day and a half from Fairbanks and, tomorrow, we'll get off the Dalton Highway.

26 June 2008

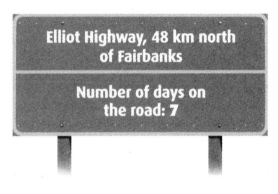

Elliot Highway, 48 km north
of Fairbanks

Number of days on
the road: 7

Number of kilometres completed: **736**

We leave the Dalton and land on another planet. The road
surfaces change dramatically. After rough gravel, tarmac is
a joy. The difference between a wild environment and a busy
highway with frequent roadside services seems surreal at
first. Over 100 kilometres of the Elliot Highway lies ahead
and, though we feel we're as good as in Fairbanks, it will be
another day and a half before we get there. But I'll take the
small victory for now; I think the Dalton has been a most
demanding challenge. We spend our last night before Fairbanks
camping on an access road just off the highway, 48 km
north of the city. Trucks and cars thunder by. Just after 11
o'clock, Alan and Brian, along with Pat, the latest recruit,
return in the jeep which Neil had left at the airport in
Fairbanks. They knew we'd be somewhere on the road
north of Fairbanks and kept their eyes peeled as they drove

back up. Pat has been in Fairbanks for the past few days and has booked us all into a hostel in the city. He's a culinary arts chef from Dublin and says he'll be happy to do a lot of the cooking for the time he'll spend with us.

Brian and Alan look as if they've been in a boxing match. Their eyes are dark blue and have huge bags underneath them, the result of the effort of getting to Fairbanks one day ahead of everyone else. At one point Brian fell asleep on the bike and crashed. The group is back together again, plus Pat, and Brian has got word that Neil is set to return in a week. Cassandra's condition is stable and she's starting treatment soon. This puts a huge spring in everyone's step. I fall asleep with a much more optimistic outlook; a confidence that, together, we'll be capable of dealing with most of what this road throws at us.

The next day, 27 June, is an easy 50 km into Fairbanks. We stop off many times along the way, eating and drinking all the things we craved for days along the Dalton. A chocolate bar or a can of Coke has never tasted so good. Cycling into Fairbanks we feel like champions.

28 June 2008

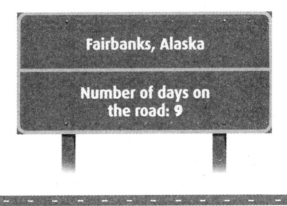

Number of kilometres completed: **786**

Fairbanks, with a population of about 35,000 people, is Alaska's second biggest city. The city is named after Charles Fairbanks, a republican senator from Indiana who became the twenty-sixth Vice President of the United States, serving from 1905 to 1909 in Teddy Roosevelt's second term. A frontier town, the original settlement was founded in 1901 when gold was discovered. Much of the city's and the greater surrounding area's history is based upon gold exploration that boomed in Alaska and in Canada's Yukon Territory during the Klondike Gold Rush of the late nineteenth century. Now the city is quite an ordinary place with none of the excitement one might associate with its history. The constant daylight makes it seem even drearier.

We stay in Billy's, a small guest house in the northern part of Fairbanks, for the day. Billy is a plump, larger than life, elderly woman who shows an interest in everyone staying in her hostel. Her daughter lived in Cork for a while, so she is particularly interested in the Irish. She visited Ireland once and says Cork was a far nicer city than Dublin.

In Billy's we meet Gunter, a travelling musician from Belgium who busked in Temple Bar for a number of years, and Joe, a native of Alaska who lives in an area about five hours west of Fairbanks, accessible only by boat, followed by an hour-long hike. I talk to Joe about Alaska and his life here. I grasp how tough the winters must be with temperatures plummeting as low as -50 °C. Joe, a man in his late forties, has lived in a cabin in the wilderness for his entire life. During the summers he collects firewood, and hunts and dries meat as well as panning for gold and selling the occasional nuggets he finds. He spends his winters surviving.

We use our free time resting, eating and chatting with other guests. The idea is to build up as much energy as possible for the week ahead. We take the bikes to a local bike store that specialises in Trek bikes, the brand we all have, and get some minor repairs done: spokes need to be replaced on some of the wheels and gears must be tightened on all of them. We also get kickstands attached, to prevent the bikes from falling over when we take breaks. Eventually, the time comes when we have to get the maps out and turn our attention to next week and another 800 km. This is what it's going to be like for the next eight months.

29 June – 1 July 2008

Last days in Alaska

Number of days on the road: 10–12

Number of kilometres completed: **1,208**

We set out to cycle towards Delta Junction, a town on a crossroads 160 km south of Fairbanks. Before we leave we have a photo call with Billy and the other guests in the hostel. We leave our email address and website at Billy's and people say they'll follow our progress as we cycle south. Since the start of the trip we've been posting video footage and blogs on our website for everyone at home to follow.

Just as we're pulling out of the hostel, someone tells us that Karl Bushby, the legendary man who is currently walking around the world, is in a café only a few blocks up the road. We make a beeline for the café.

We've heard of Bushby. He's been walking around the world since 1998 and estimates that he'll be back in England by 2014. He has already crossed the Bering Sea between the USA and Russia (he and the Frenchman who joined him are the first people to do so) by hopping between ice floes but he was refused entry and sent back to Alaska by the Russian authorities: Bushby was found with GPS equipment, which is prohibited and the gun he needed for self-defence against polar bears. He was arrested, put on trial for spying and deported. He started his journey in Tierra del Fuego and has already walked up much of the route we intend to cycle down. It would be exciting to get him on camera and hear some advice.

We arrive at the café and look around. The place is empty. According to the waitress, we've missed Bushby by ten minutes.

We push it hard on the second week and increase the daily mileage in order to make back the day we lost at the beginning of the first week. Although we've said that this trip is not a race, in a way it is because we want to keep up with our own planned itinerary. Our second week in Alaska is in direct contrast with our first. The two halves of Alaska seem like two different worlds.

The road south of Fairbanks towards Canada is immaculate and has an abundance of service stations, camping sites, Recreational Vehicle parks and fast-food joints sprinkled down both sides of the highway. It's amazing how such small luxuries become so important. Last week I daydreamed for hours about drinking a can of Coke. The relative ease of the second week is a relief and there are far fewer mosquitoes. The horrible sores all over everyone's bodies are given a chance to heal.

Pat is beginning his first day. Riding out of Fairbanks, he watches the movie *300*, an epic set in Ancient Greece and starring Gerard Butler, on a DVD player mounted on the handlebars of his bike. Some of us occasionally listen to music while cycling but watching a movie is taking things to the next level. Pat arrived in Fairbanks tipping the scales at a little over 15 stone and some of the group are worried that he won't make the daily distances. During the middle of his first day he disappears for an hour.

'Where were you, Pat?' asks someone, when he catches us up eventually .

'Just taking a small nap in a bush a few miles back.'

We make quick time down the road, staying in Cathedral Rapids on the 29th before passing through Tok. On 30 June, we stay in a campsite in the Native American village of Northway, 6 km north of the Canadian border. We're starting to learn how to work together on the bikes, breaking the headwind for each other. Last week we were all too strung out along the road to do this. We're fitter now. We each take a mile at the front of the line, everyone else files in behind and then we rotate the position after every mile post. It brings about a very quick pace and makes the cycling much easier.

Everyone is in great form. We have plenty of time to sit around the campfire in the evenings, chat or do a bit of reading. I've started *The Count of Monte Cristo*.

As we approach the Canadian border, we're about 1,200 km from Deadhorse and have been on the road for nearly two weeks. Reaching Canada and the border crossing makes me realise, for the first time, that we are capable of covering huge distances on the bikes. Before I started the trip, I had no real concept of these distances, of what it would feel like to cycle 1,200 km. When we reach the border there is a great sense of progression. But the highway in Canada is almost twice as long as the highway in Alaska and, after that, we need to cycle through the USA and Mexico; three huge countries that won't even bring us to the halfway point.

CANADA

2 July 2008

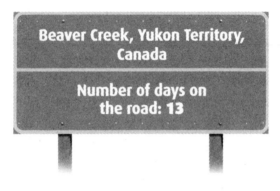

Beaver Creek, Yukon Territory, Canada

Number of days on the road: 13

Number of kilometres completed: **1,244**

The American and Canadian border offices lie 30 km apart and the road between them is unpaved gravel – big stones and pebbles. We enter Canada and the Yukon Territory. Named after the River Yukon that flows within its boundaries, Yukon is the westernmost and smallest of Canada's three federal territories. Half of the 3,500-km-long river flows within Alaska where it empties into the Bering Sea. When translated from the local native tongue of Gwich'in, Yukon means 'Great River'. The territory is the approximate shape of a right angle triangle and borders North-West Territories to the west and British Columbia to the south. The vast majority of Alaska's eastern boundary and contact with Canada is with the Yukon. The sparsely populated territory abounds with snowmelt lakes and perennially snow-capped mountains.

The first town we reach after from Tok in Alaska is Beaver Creek. It is the most western of all Canadian settlements, a fact stated on a sign as you enter the village. We stop at the restaurant and order bacon double cheeseburgers and pitchers of beer. (So much for the protein shakes and complex carbohydrates.) There's one of those funny-looking Mounties with a wide brimmed hat walking around the place. It turns out he's not a cop at all but a character in a cultural play that's going on in a theatre in the village.

The most noticeable difference between Alaska and Yukon Territory is the prices. It's expensive this far north in Canada and much more so than in Alaska. A packet of cigarettes can be up to $18 and general groceries are very dear too. It costs a huge amount to transport anything this far north, we're told. I find out from our waiter that the locals, and particularly the Native people, use their right to hunt their own meat such as elk, muscot and caribou, since the cost of buying lean meat in the supermarkets is so high.

We're paying for this trip ourselves so we're trying to keep costs as low as possible. We employ a kitty system for the buying of petrol for the jeep, for food and for all our other communal items.

We spend our first night in Canada in Suang campsite, on the banks of a lake, 16 km south of Beaver Creek. I walk down to the water to wash. The still water mirrors the purple snow-capped mountain that stands behind it. The light is changing. Real darkness hasn't fallen yet but a dusk of sorts is beginning to descend at night.

We're well into the second week of cycling and seem to be getting the hang of the daily routine. We get up at around 8 every morning. Alan, who's usually the first out of the tent, makes porridge and, when it's ready, the rest of us emerge from the tents and gulp it back. After breakfast, before taking off, there are jobs to do such as rolling up the sleeping mattresses, taking down the tents, putting away the camp chairs and repacking the trailer. It takes about two hours from the time we wake up until the time we get going. There's a good bit of hanging around in the mornings and, because it doesn't get dark, there's no urgency within the group to arrive early at the daily destination. We're still very much operating on our own clock.

We take a break every 25 km, stopping for lunch after about 70 or 80 km depending on the distance for the whole day. Ideally, we like to stop for lunch a little past the halfway mark for the day since, psychologically, it's easier then to finish the day out. But circumstances change constantly. Every night when we get into camp we split the jobs to be done and before anyone has a shower or sits down for the rest of the evening, the tents are up, the mattresses rolled out and the food prepared. It's going well and ought to become more efficient as time goes on.

Yukon Territory has a mixture of excellent and appalling road surfaces. In the summer months of every year there are heavy roadworks, since the road breaks up every spring when the ice melts. The constant freezing and thawing of the roads' surfaces, as the seasons change, causes extensive damage. It means that there are large stretches of unpaved surfaces under construction and long waits because traffic is often made to stop for a single lane system. The difference the quality of road surface makes to progress and also to your state of mind is profound. On poor surfaces progress is cut almost in half and it feels as though you're going nowhere. The uneven, stony surfaces hurt your bike and eventually you feel it in your limbs, back and neck. I thought I was done with this torture after the Dalton. Cycling on these surfaces is like cycling a jackhammer all day. On bad stretches you dream of better surfaces. You swear to yourself that you can't do another stretch on the rough stuff and then, out of nowhere, 5 km of stones appear around the corner. It becomes a battle between cyclist and the road.

As we approach a bridge over a small river, about 50 metres away, we see a grizzly bear plodding along the road. We quietly dismount and watch. The bear eventually crosses over to the other side and out of sight. I get back on the bike and, when I come to the point where the bear crossed, look to the right and see it, sitting in a dip off the road, not very far away, staring back at me. This is my first encounter with a bear; he's young and affable with a lovely golden brown coat.

The grizzlies of Canada attract tourists. When we bump into people, they tell us about the bears they've encountered along the road but we haven't seen all that many yet. Apparently, tourists have been getting out of their cars and throwing food at the bears. The locals hate this because it makes the animals more accustomed to humans and ultimately more dangerous. Tourists view the bears as attractions but the locals know better.

After another 8 km, Brian and I find ourselves ahead of the rest, cycling through a landscape that is free of even the most basic settlements. Brian has tremendous energy and is always a great man to have a chat with on the bike. He's a very personable character. He has the 'gift of the gab' in spades and I know this will be a great asset for the group on the way down the road.

We cross over a long bridge, below which we see dozens of horses drinking at the river. I suspect they're wild because they gallop away once they see us. On the other side of the bridge we find a small convenience store. We're looking for chocolate, a cold drink and, if we're lucky, even a sandwich. We walk in, have a look around and see an elderly couple sitting inside. The man, aged about seventy, polishes figurines while the woman lies on a sunlounger and reads. On the shelves are cans of peas and tuna dating from years before. Other shelves are full of knick-knacks and small figures but there's almost nothing worth buying.

'Excuse me, have you any sandwiches by any chance, or a can of Coke?'

A couple of cans of 'pop' are produced from a fridge somewhere out of sight. We have a chat and I get the impression that the couple lack even a basic knowledge of current affairs. They say the last time they went down to Whitehorse, the territory's capital, they ate at a restaurant called Kentucky Fried Chicken. The old-timer asks me if I have ever heard of KFC, adding that the chicken was the best he's ever had. Yukon is about eight times the size of Ireland but has a population of a little over 30,000 people. It's one of the most sparsely populated areas on the planet.

Our second day off from cycling is on 4 July and we spend it in Haines Junction, a village on the western periphery of

Kluane National Park and Reserve, itself an area of some 22,000 square kilometres on the extreme southwestern corner of Yukon. The park includes Mount Logan, which, at 5,959 metres, is the highest mountain in Canada. Mountains and glaciers dominate the park's landscape and it is home to dozens of protected species of animals and birds, including the Golden Eagle. This wildly beautiful area was declared a UNESCO world heritage site in 1979.

The campsite is at the entrance to Haines Junction and run by a man with an accent that reminds me of the television show *Seinfeld*. The New York accent is a refreshing surprise. The village is surrounded by mountains which continually change colour. When the sun is bright they give off shades of pink or orange and in the evenings they cast dark shadows.

While Haines Junction isn't quite a one-horse town, you'll find the major buildings – a petrol station, a restaurant, a police station and a supermarket – at the same crossroads. This is still the biggest community we've come across for hundreds of kilometres. Having spent the past two weeks in a wilderness, Haines Junction seems like an urban metropolis. We order pizza, buy beer and sit around the tents in the campsite. We feel chuffed to be 1,600 km down the road. Within the group there's quiet satisfaction – that's more than twice the length of Ireland, all the way from Mizen to Malin and back again. Alan, Brian and John will drive to Haines, in Alaska, tomorrow to collect Neil who is flying back from Boston. With Neil returning, the trip as it was planned will start only now.

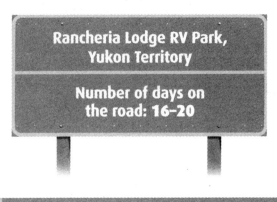

Number of kilometres completed: **2,076**

The cycling in northern Canada is made up of long tough days. The roads follow the shapes of lakes and loop up and down steep river valleys that are covered in thick coniferous forestry. Streams and rivers flow loudly and a smell of fresh wet pine needles fills the moist air. The absence of people and dwellings makes the environment feel even more natural and wild. Maybe the old folks back in the not-so-convenient convenience store have the right philosophy, living out in the middle of nowhere like old frontier folk, with few of the problems we have grown used to.

Before we get Week 3 underway we look at the map and see a series of rivers immediately ahead. This means there'll be a good deal of climbing and then descending into river valleys. Cycling over 160 km a day, we bypass Whitehorse, which accounts for two-thirds of Yukon's population. We cycle on through the village of Teslin and on the third night of the third week stop in Rancheria Lodge and Campground.

When I sit down in the lodge, it seems as if we haven't been off the bikes all week. We're aiming to do 880 km this week and so, the deal is, if we want to take a rest day at the end of it, the average over six days will have to increase. I want to eat but most of all I want to relax on my own for ten or fifteen minutes and gather my thoughts. If anyone's feeling sick, tired or annoyed with things, the best thing to do is to sort it out quietly yourself rather than dumping your problem on to the group. These periods come and go and easy weeks seem to follow tough ones.

After breakfast the following morning, it is decided to cycle 190 km in order to get out of Yukon Territory and off the Alaskan highway. We'll cycle into British Columbia and this will be the longest day of the journey yet. My energy is low. I put it to the lads that we don't want to burn ourselves out but the general mood is that another big day is the best thing to do.

The morning turns out to be very manageable. A day's difficulty rarely depends on its distance but rather on what the weather is like and the road conditions. With a strong tail wind and excellent surfaces we make fast progress to our turn-off point. We cycle 100 km in three hours. When there are steep, short inclines followed by long-drawn-out descents, it is extremely quick and we can get up to an average speed of around 30 km/h.

At a crossroads we pull into a petrol station and have our last lunch before we leave the Alaskan Highway and enter the Cassier Highway. Neil has just finished preparing lunch and is surprised at how quickly we have covered the distance. We are turning off because we're heading towards Vancouver. The Cassier Highway is a narrower, hillier but much quieter road: we can cycle two or three abreast and chat, which we couldn't really do on the Alaskan. Shortly after turning on to the Cassier, we enter British Columbia. A sign reads, 'Welcome to British Columbia, the most beautiful place on earth' followed by *Splendor Sine Occasu*, (Splendour without Diminishment).

A river valley cuts through the Cassier Mountains and then curves around a huge lake that shows the perfect symmetry of the forest and mountains it reflects. I watch a Golden Eagle hunting a smaller bird. On the grassy verges off the sides of the road we see black bears, dozens of elk and caribou. John sees a wolf dash across the road.

Our first night in BC is spent in a campsite on the shore of Boya Lake. The lake is a mix of green on its edges and blue in the deeper middle. Two Golden Eagles swoop high above the tree line, screeching as they glide. You can see the white tips of their wings and their golden beaks. A long jetty runs into the lake and we have good fun jumping off it. Pat screams his head off while doing naked dive-bombs. We roar and shout because there is a good echo and because we're the only people here. This week we have cycled over 160 km every day.

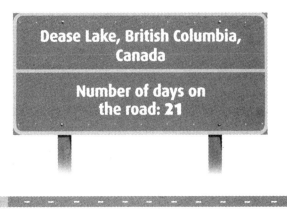

Dease Lake, British Columbia, Canada

Number of days on the road: 21

Number of kilometres completed: **2,435**

It's the last day of this cycling week: we've taken to counting the beginning of our week as the first day of cycling after a break and the end as the day we stop for some well-deserved time off. Ahead of us on the road we can see another cyclist. It's a woman! We've seen more black bears than women over the past three weeks. Her name is Jennine, she tells us, when we catch up. She's about thirty, comes from Seattle and is headed for Haines, Alaska (not to be confused with Haines Junction, Canada). The city of Haines is situated in the narrow portion of Alaska that runs south, alongside Canada's western border.

Cillian has been complaining about the lack of people – women, in particular – we've encountered, so the rest of us cycle on towards Dease Lake, leaving the two to become acquainted. We're taking a day off tomorrow, so I'm keen to finish the day and get off the bike as quickly as possible.

After lunch the cycling is difficult. The road brings us on to appalling surfaces of mud and gravel and we end up strung out along the road. Each of us battles through the rest of the day on our own and eventually we arrive at Dease Lake. We've now done five 160-km days in a row. Cillian and Jennine come into camp long after everyone else.

We invite Jennine to join us for dinner. She says the purpose of her trip is to mourn the recent death by suicide of her best friend. She talks about how difficult the past few months have been for her. It seems her reason for being on the road is very different to our own. Generally, the mood in our camp is upbeat; we put on music and dance around the car every morning to warm up. We don't take ourselves very seriously. We tell Jennine she's welcome to join us on the road for a while. She says she'd like to tag along for a few days until our routes diverge. Perhaps we can cheer her up.

We take a day off at Dease Lake. It is another tiny community. Canada is the world's second largest country by total area but most of the population is clustered alongside the American border. The rest of the country is like Dease Lake and the surrounding environment; vast and empty of people.

The lake for which this community is named lies only a few kilometres from Dease Lake village but, according to the barman we met last night, the lake is polluted with effluent from logging machines and not worth a visit. I've seen enough lakes over the past three weeks and would rather relax and recharge the batteries instead.

Recharging the batteries means eating and indulging in as little physical exertion as possible. The binge eating is

Day 24 We keep our distance from one of the many dangerous log trailers we come across in British Columbia, Canada.

phenomenal. Entire packets of biscuits aren't shared and two main courses is now normal. We snack constantly, eating anything we can get our hands on. We're burning four thousand calories a day, so we can eat whatever and whenever we want. Initially, we monitored what we ate, being careful to be healthy but now it's a case of quantity rather than quality. There's nothing much else to do anyway. There are two hotels, a restaurant and a gift shop.

From what I've seen in BC, the big industry is timber and logging. BC's economy has gone through dramatic boom and bust periods over the decades, depending on the price of timber and demand for it and other natural resources. In fact, this history is evident throughout the country in general and we have passed through entirely abandoned villages. Timber is the main business, especially this far north. The trees are cut using giant machines that grab the tree, cut it at its base and then remove its branches in a matter of minutes. The machines roar like dinosaurs throughout the forests. It's strange to think this was all once done by dozens of people with manual saws.

Lorry-loads of stripped trees rattle by us daily; the tail swings of their trailers are a constant threat when they turn corners. We have cycled by huge fields of fresh stumps like headstones in enormous graveyards. Timber is the life of the local economies and one of the only reasons why anyone lives here.

11–13 July 2008

Bell 2, British Columbia

Number of days on
the road: 22–23

Number of kilometres completed: **2,720**

Before we leave Dease Lake, we have to make a couple of decisions about the road ahead. Our next stop – over six days away – is scheduled to be in Prince George. This town, as the crow flies, is a long way off course. We don't discover that there is an alternative to our planned route until we meet the chef of the restaurant where we've just eaten our $25-a-head breakfast. The chef tells us we'd be 'f***ing crazy' to cycle to Prince George if it's Vancouver we want to go to. His advice is to cycle the western route to Prince Rupert and then take the ferry from there to Vancouver Island. After we cycle down the island, another short ferry journey will take us directly across to the city of Vancouver, he says.

This plan sounds better than the other route which initially goes northeast. Changing the route will mean that we'll have more time off in Vancouver but when Neil rings the ferry company to reserve a spot for our jeep, they say they're booked out.

I'm already imagining a comfortable bed in Vancouver and what I'll do with our extended free time. Surely there must be space? Alan rings the ferry company and it turns out there are a couple of spaces available but for oversized vehicles only. The solution is simple, we'll just stack a number of boxes on top of the jeep and make it oversized. The ferry company doesn't object to this ruse, so we book ourselves on board.

The change of plan infuses us with enthusiasm. There's something more exciting about cycling towards the coast rather than back inland. Cycling on the Cassier Highway is enjoyable. It isn't a surprise to see a black bear anymore: they laze around, just off the sides of the roads. As they plod, trying to exert as little energy as possible, you wonder how they could harm anyone.

On 12 July, in a campsite another couple of hundred kilometres closer to Prince Rupert, a tall bloke with long hair and wearing shades comes over looking for a pump. We must be any solo cyclist's dream with our trailer full of repair equipment and spare gear. He tells us his name is Marcus.

'Where are you coming from?' asks Brian.

'Riding from Anchorage, on my way home to Vancouver,' says Marcus.

He tells us he's been working for the Discovery Channel in Alaska, filming wilderness survival expert Bear Grylls, a well-known television star. When filming finished up, Marcus fancied riding a friend's bike home to Vancouver.

'Most of the filming is done from the side of the road, and Bear has a PA who follows him around with an instant latte machine,' says Marcus, 'but he eats all the raw salmon for real.'

'We're on our way to Vancouver if you fancy tagging along?' Alan says.

Marcus throws his pannier bags with his gear in the boot of the jeep and we get back on the road together. As it turns out, he's not only a brilliant cyclist but a representative skier and a mountain climber as well. On the tough, uphill climbs, he takes off from everyone else in a flash. There's no point in trying to keep up with him but I am learning from his technique. About 2,400 km in and I'm still finding out the best way to cycle properly. At no stage is Marcus ever in the top gears, struggling or straining against the bike. Rather, he uses the lower, easier gears and maintains a faster, more fluid momentum. He says this creates less muscle fatigue, meaning one can last longer on the bike. I try the new method and, although it takes a bit of time to get used to, eventually it feels better. Marcus also gives me a few pointers about body position and gear changing.

We cycle up to ten hours every day and time can fly or it can drag slowly. Ten straight hours every day is a lot to spend in one's own company. Sometimes it seems like there are two people on the bike; the body cycling but the mind somewhere far away thinking about something else: ex-girlfriends, college, family, the future. During long stretches, in extreme cases, body and mind can become so detached that you can forget you're on the bike. You can fall into a trance-like state that can be strange but also enjoyable.

Today there's a long, flat stretch and, while the body

continues to pedal, I wonder how the next eight months will unfold. I imagine myself being in the countries we plan to cycle through. I imagine the different terrains and people; all a big mystery. Before I left Ireland, my only approach to this journey was to take it one day at a time. I figured I wouldn't make it to the end of the road if I approached it any other way; it's just too long. But sometimes, like today, the challenges that lie ahead creep into my mind. How different is it going to be in the deserts of Baja and Atacama? What will it be like when we cycle through Mexico and it gets more dangerous? It's important to snap out of letting your mind drift like this, since the size of the journey could potentially overwhelm and get the better of you.

On the evening of 13 July we camp at Bell 2, the biggest heli-skiing resort in the world. In the winter months, for $10,000 a weekend, you can catch a helicopter up here from Vancouver and be dropped on top of a mountain with a pair of skis as often as you like.

Bell 2 is a collection of luxurious pine chalets in the mountains. We pass up the chalets for a couple of campsites hidden away behind the complex. There's a shop and a restaurant at the front of the resort. We sit outside and have an ice cream. Helicopters land and take off 50 metres away, to the side of the hotel, creating a continuous plume of light dust. There are a few bikers around, walking about in their leathers, and six or seven Harleys parked outside. One of the bikers comes over to us.

'I don't understand you guys. Wouldn't you just prefer to jump on a Harley?' he says.

He rolls his wrist like he's twisting an accelerator when

he says 'Harley'. We bump into bikers the whole time. They're cool guys but the truth is, I've never felt like jumping on a Harley. Think of what the bikers are missing as they storm through tiny villages in a cloud of smoke where we might have stopped for a chat with a local. This just wouldn't be the same trip on a motorcycle.

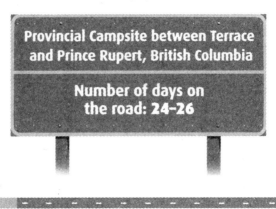

Provincial Campsite between Terrace and Prince Rupert, British Columbia

Number of days on the road: 24–26

Number of kilometres completed: **3,043**

Marcus' original plan, like our own, was to ride through Prince George rather than Prince Rupert, since it's quite expensive to catch the ferry. However, he seems to be having good fun with us, so he decides to change his plan and stick around. He's coming out of his shell as the days go on. Jennine, on the other hand, after staying with us for five days, takes off alone again and we wish her all the best.

We arrive at a crossroads in Kitwanga, leave the Cassier Highway and set out on the tail end of the Yellowhead Highway. The Yellowhead is a major east-to-west highway connecting the four western Canadian provinces of BC, Alberta, Saskatchewan and Manitoba. The highway is named after the Yellowhead Pass, the route the road takes when it crosses the Rockies. I'm sad to leave the Cassier. The road has been our home for the past ten days and has given us such a great impression of British Columbia. I'm beginning to believe the province's own slogan that this is the most beautiful place on earth.

The Yellowhead follows the course of the Skeena River, which flows all the way to the Pacific. Whenever a river flows in the direction you're cycling, progress is fast because the road goes downhill with the river. A train whistles by, making the progress seem even faster still.

We stop for lunch on the outskirts of the town of Terrace. Over lunch, Cillian informs us that he has decided to go the whole way to the tip of Argentina. He, like John, had planned to go home from San Diego but now he has changed his mind. Only Alan, Kev, Brian and myself had committed to cycling all the way to the end of the road. We're delighted with Cillian's decision. John wants to continue to the end too but his case is less straightforward because he still has another year to run in college. We've been encouraging Cillian since the start to stay on but it can't have been an easy call for him to make. I think he surprised himself that he got this far as comfortably as he has done. Right now, I don't know what my decision would be if I were Cillian. His trip has just jumped from a 9,000-km summer break to a 25,000-km, nine-month affair.

We want to put ourselves in range of Prince Rupert tomorrow since the ferry leaves very early the next morning. We leave Terrace and cycle another 60 km to a provincial national park. The Skeena flows alongside, to our left. The park, a couple of kilometres off the road, is right beside a tributary of the Skeena, which trickles through steep mountains. There is a waterfall on the other side of the river. I jump in for a wash and wade over to a sandbank that divides the river. When I call out to some of the others on the bank to come in, my voice echoes against the mountains.

After we pitch our tents and cook a meal, there is no sign of Marcus. He's by far the strongest cyclist of the group and must have bolted on ahead before Neil decided where we were crashing for the night.

'Who in their right mind would put up with us for this long? It didn't take Jennine that long to leave, did it?' asks Alan.

But of course we have Marcus' panniers. The joking eventually changes to concern. Two of the lads jump in the jeep and search for 15 km up and down the road but find nothing. There's not much chat that night; nobody wants to contemplate what might have happened to our friend.

17 July 2008

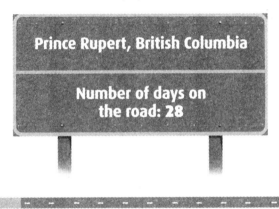

Prince Rupert, British Columbia

Number of days on
the road: 28

Number of kilometres completed: **3,168**

The next morning at 7 a.m., as we're pulling out, Marcus cycles back up the road towards us.

'Jeez, I didn't know where you guys were,' he says.

We're as relieved as he is: it's a horrible feeling getting lost on the road. It happened to me on a training ride in Ireland, quite late at night. Your head runs wild thinking of all the possible things that might have happened. Did the others pull up short? Did someone get injured? Last night Marcus went on ahead; the entrance to the park is so concealed that he just missed it. He ended up sleeping in a public toilet at a picnic area. This is life on the road: unpredictable, dirty and basic.

In a much tighter group we ride towards Prince Rupert, the hub of BC's north coast. The weather turns bad and the river opens up, widening into an enormous estuary. The landscape flattens out. A thick sea mist descends and the temperature plummets. The ferry leaves at 5 in the morning, so we camp at an RV park close to the port. It's the first time for us to get off the bikes knowing we'll have a break from cycling for the next few days at least. We haven't had two days in a row without cycling for nearly a month.

It is two days short of a month since we cycled out of Deadhorse and I can't make up my mind whether it feels like a long time ago or not. My body clock has become muddled. I don't know if the distance we've covered feels like a lot or just a small part of a bigger picture. I need space to recharge physically and mentally.

There will be time to take a break in Vancouver. A few more friends are coming out to join us, so we'll have to wait for them there anyway. We've cycled nearly 3,200 km to get to Prince Rupert and it shows. Our equipment, the inside of the trailer and the bikes are filthy. Things that were once stored neatly in boxes are now strewn around the back of the jeep. Some of the bikes require repairs. Everything needs a good scrub, including ourselves.

It will take seventeen hours to get from Prince Rupert to Port Hardy, the port town at the northern end of Vancouver Island. We take a four-berth cabin, so we can take turns catching up on sleep. It was an early start this morning but it's also the first time we've had the opportunity to sleep on a bed since Fairbanks, the first time we've been able to rest our heads against pillows rather than rolled up jumpers. Words can't describe how comfortable the bed feels. I fall into a long and deep sleep.

After three hours I turn the bed over to John and walk up to the top deck. It's the first time I've worn my jeans in quite some time and they're falling down around my hips: I've lost about a stone in weight since Alaska and I can see it in my face when I catch a glimpse of myself in a mirror while walking through the lobby of the ferry. Up on deck, on the stern of the boat, I look back at the white wake. The ferry hugs the coastline going south. There's no open water to the west because a continuous series of islands follows the route all the way to Vancouver Island. The ferry snakes down past the rugged coastline, threading through the islands. From the deck we can see frontier communities, originally set up along the mainland, that have been abandoned and rotting for decades.

Vancouver Island is one of several North American regions named after George Vancouver, the British naval officer who explored these waters between 1791 and 1794. The island is only 400 km long, so we can take our time riding down before crossing back over to Vancouver. For once, we won't be racing against the clock.

It's late when we get off the ferry and there's no room at any of the campsites in Port Hardy. We pitch the tents on a grassy verge in front of a factory, just outside the town. No more beds; back to normality.

19 July 2008

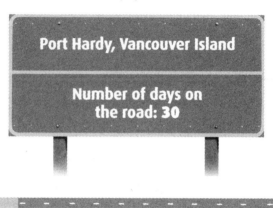

Port Hardy, Vancouver Island

Number of days on
the road: 30

Number of kilometres completed: **3,298**

Marcus takes off early. He figures it will take him two days to get back home to Vancouver. That's fast cycling, even by his standards. He gives us his number and invites us all to stay in his house when we get there.

Port Hardy is in the middle of 'FILOMI Days', its annual celebrations. FILOMI stands for the first two letters in Fishing, Logging and Mining. We manage to get ourselves off the side of the road and into a campsite nearer town. The celebrations are in full swing. There's an outdoor fête with pony rides, roller hockey games and dozens of stalls selling sweets and popcorn. There are kids everywhere and the place is a hive of excitement. Cillian and I stroll down town for a beer and a game of pool.

Vancouver Island seems like a different world to the British Columbia we've already passed through. In Yukon

Territory and northern BC we'd often cycle for hours and not see a single soul. Vancouver Island is a holiday destination for people from the city and beyond. There are golf courses and holiday villages. Cars full of families pass us all the time. The ferry has delivered us back to a more familiar reality. The pace of life seems frantic in comparison to that of the past month.

We cycle by five-star hotels and shopping malls. Money oozes from the place. We pass expensive fish restaurants and beach bars and I wonder if we're still in British Columbia at all. The campsites we stop in are full of holidaymakers and children's camps. This is a far more convenient way for us to travel, with better roads and lots of services, but it's not the Canada I'd been growing to love. I miss Yukon Territory, northern BC and, dare I say, the Dalton Highway as well. There will be more challenges ahead, in even remoter parts of the world than Alaska or Yukon.

Vancouver, British Columbia

Number of days on the road: 31–39

Number of kilometres completed: **3,682**

Vancouver is an important milestone for us. For the first time, people at home express genuine shock that we've cycled to Vancouver from northern Alaska: not many people know where Whitehorse, Dease Lake or Prince Rupert are on the map but they know where Vancouver is. On previous weekends, when I had called family or friends, though we had covered exactly the same distances that week and possibly even more, the fact that we were in Tok or Haines Junction didn't excite anyone.

'Wow, I can't believe you're in Vancouver. You've come so far,' my mother says.

We stay with Marcus in Deep Cove, a wealthy suburb. Initially, we're anxious that there are far too many of us but when we get to his house, we realise that we needn't have worried. Marcus, who has been sleeping rough through

Canada for the past two weeks, lives with his parents in an enormous, four-storey house set in a large garden. We're warmly welcomed by his parents, Judy and Daniel, who thank us for 'looking after Marcus while he was on the road'.

Marcus shows us to his basement, which is carpeted and warm and where there are plenty of camp beds and mattresses. His mother prepares a meal for us and gives us free rein in her home.

We have to wait a few days in Vancouver for Anthony, Eric, Tom and Mike to arrive for the next leg of the journey. The lads have each agreed to raise €2,000 for our charity in exchange for doing a stint on the trip. Meanwhile, Marcus organises kayaking in the nearby cove, a trip to the cinema to see the latest *Batman* movie and arranges parties and nights out with his friends.

Two nights before we leave, a firework display, called 'Celebration of Light', takes place in the city harbour. It's actually a firework competition between the US, Canada, Japan and China. Along with some of Marcus' friends, we watch the fireworks from a small beach that looks back on the city. Every spare inch of viewing ground is occupied.

People here have a fantastic outdoors lifestyle. With the ski resort of Whistler only a couple of hours to the east and an enormous coastline to the west, this part of the world is an active person's Mecca.

USA

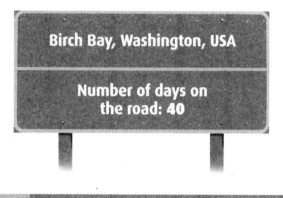

Birch Bay, Washington, USA

Number of days on the road: 40

Number of kilometres completed: **3,771**

Marcus and his friend Chad, who has just cycled home to Vancouver from Toronto on a mountain bike, guide us out of the city towards the American border. We're a far bigger group leaving the city. Eric, Tom, Mike and Anthony have come out to join us for this leg of the trip down the west coast of the States. All are in their early twenties. Tom, an actor and friend of Kev's from England, went to college in Trinity. Eric is from Dublin but goes to the University of Wisconsin. Mike is a friend of Eric's from college and is from San Diego. Anthony is a good friend of Brian's from Dublin. The newcomers have the fantastic start-of-journey energy I remember we all had last month. They're amazed that we've cycled this far already. I can tell they're taking confidence from our own progress.

We're now eleven cyclists, which presents more difficult logistical problems. It takes a long time to leave the city and find the right road that will take us south towards the US border.

It's pouring rain as we say our goodbyes to Marcus and Chad. Vancouver and the state of Washington are notorious for the quick, heavy downpours that come in rapidly from the Pacific. Cycling in the rain, with poor visibility, slicker, more dangerous surfaces, sodden gear and the spray-back from the rear wheel of the bike or vehicle in front is unpleasant. As we try and find our way south, the support jeep takes a wrong turn and drives towards a different border crossing. Mistakenly, the group then splits into two and goes in different directions. Punctures delay us even further. Things would have been easier to handle two weeks ago in northern BC because instructions in the morning would have sounded something like, 'Right, lads stay on this road and head south for a couple of days.'

We head towards Washington on the interstate, the busiest and most direct route, but thick with traffic. Cars and trucks thunder by at top speed. It's illegal and dangerous for us to be on this road but we just can't find an alternative.

Somehow, we all manage to reconvene at the US border. Everyone is drenched. Known as the International Boundary, the Canadian-American border is officially the longest land border in the world. In the mid-nineteenth century, this part of North America was called 'Oregon Country' by the Americans but the 'Columbia District' by the British. The border was the subject of years of dispute, with both powers having territorial and commercial aspirations in the region. The area of the disputed region was made up of all territory west of the Rockies, north of the 42nd parallel and south of parallel 54°40' North.

We cross from Surrey in BC to Blaine in Washington. A 'Peace Arch' stands between the two countries. The monument has the flags of the United States and Canada mounted on its crown and inscriptions on both sides of its frieze. The inscription on the Canadian side reads 'Brethren Dwelling Together in Peace', while on the US side it reads 'Children of a Common Mother'. Another inscription reads, 'May These Gates Never be Closed'.

We get our passports stamped and fill out the Homeland Security Emigration control forms.

Purpose of Journey: Transitory
Ultimate Destination: Tierra del Fuego

This is our fourth crossing of an American border in five weeks.

We spin on south, passing beneath an enormous 'Stars and Stripes'. Almost every home and business has a flag flying outside it. The group has become unwieldy; we're like a breakaway peloton of a road race. The new additions are still getting into the swing of things and I can't imagine that coming out of Vancouver in the rain was an easy start for them.

It's sunny and peaceful in the American countryside. The rain has stopped. We cycle on quiet roads through a couple of sleepy villages before we set up camp in Birch Bay, a small seaside resort that looks out over the Georgia Strait, the section of ocean between the mainland and Vancouver Island. The first day of a new week always seems to be a bit disorganised; we'll have to come up with a more effective way of moving a bigger group in future.

30 July–3 August 2008

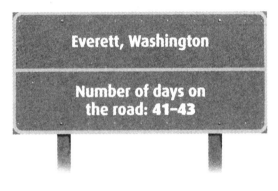

Everett, Washington

Number of days on
the road: 41–43

Number of kilometres completed: **3,906**

We continue south towards Everett, a suburb of northern Seattle. Just when we think we've reached a maximum number of cyclists we collect another two in Everett. Killian and Bryan are two friends from Dublin who are in America for the summer. They've been working with a furniture removal company but were delighted to quit their jobs and do some cycling instead. It wasn't a very hard sell: want to lift pianos for the rest of the summer or spin down Highway 101 for a couple of weeks?

Having spent nearly a week in Vancouver, I'm keen to start getting big distances in again and regain the momentum. When the going seems tough, we know we're making progress and at the moment things feel just that bit too easy.

On 1 August we decide to split up and ride through Seattle in two groups, a tactic we hope will make our passage easier. It's disappointing that we won't be spending any time in Seattle since it's a city I've wanted to check out. I'm a big *Fraiser* fan. Riding towards the town humming, 'Baby I hear the blues are calling tossed salads and scrambled eggs', I see the 'Space Needle', the unusual, narrow-looking tower with the rotating disc-like top, sticking out from all the other buildings.

Our plan to divide the group doesn't work. A series of punctures and wrong turns stops progress. It's complicated to get through Seattle because the map is unclear. We're not sure what route we should take. Very quickly, we disperse throughout the city in threes and fours. Brian's left crank, the part of the bike that joins together the pedal and the bicycle, comes off. Then more punctures. Tom, who joined the group in Vancouver, has five punctures in the space of only a few hours. I ask a number of people for directions and get different answers from each one. Brian battles on with one pedal and we take turns pushing him up any hills along the way. I can't help laughing as I see Eric and Killian pushing Brian up a hill. We're on our way to Argentina, didn't you know?

By evening, half the group is still missing but I suppose they're thinking the same thing about our group. The urban sprawl of Seattle continues for miles and, behind, the first signs of the night skyline begin to show. We have to call it a day. We get as far as South Tacoma, a suburb, and find a motel. Neil drives around the city rounding up as many lost cyclists as possible. He comes across Tom and Pat, who have spent the past few hours in a pub.

'I just gave up, man, I didn't know where anyone was, so I just went for a beer,' says Pat.

We decide we have to come up with better daily plans. We must choose our routes more clearly and, most importantly, let everyone know the route plan before we head out. Alan is the man who picks the roads and comes up with the daily destination and this is not an easy task in a big city or in suburban areas. Outside our motel in South Tacoma the group gathers together. We decide we'll cycle as far as Elma, 128 km down the road, taking a more southwesterly direction towards the Pacific. At first, we'll have to cycle on Interstate 5 again, meaning more heavy traffic and punctures. At Elma, we'll be within 48 km of Highway 101, the road that we'll take down most of the US.

'Let's all stick together,' says Brian.

Most people listen to the daily route plan but Pat has other ideas. He takes off every morning with his own plan for the day in his head.

'Did you get those details for today, Pat?' Brian asks.

'Yeh no bother, man.'

More punctures on the interstate. Shards of glass and debris from car crashes easily pierce our tyres, which are not as strong and thick as when we started. When one of us has a puncture, we try and get the whole group to stop in order to keep everyone together. After 16 km or so of good progress, bright blue lights flash behind us and a voice, which gets louder by the second, booms from a megaphone.

'This is an interstate highway. Please pull over at the next exit. You are not permitted to cycle on the interstate.'

We pull over and gather together. The police car stops 5 metres ahead of us, its lights flashing furiously. The officer then emerges from his car, places a wide-brimmed hat on his head and paces grimly back towards us.

'Jaysus, we're in trouble now,' Brian whispers.

'Officer, I hope there's no problem here,' he begins. Brian is usually the first of us to step forward in such situations.

'What are you guys doing on my interstate?' the cop asks in an unexpectedly high-pitched voice.

'Sorry, officer, but we're looking to get to Elma,' says Alan.

'Are you aware that it's an offence to bike on the interstate?'

'We weren't sure. We're very sorry.'

He asks us for our names and we apologise abjectly as he writes them down. His radio crackles intermittently with the voices of other cops. He wipes his brow.

'I'm going to let you guys off this time,' he says, eventually. 'I got Irish heritage.'

His name is Highway Patrolman Erik Thomas and he says he also wants to help us because his name includes the names of two of our group; Eric and Tom. He leads us off the highway and on to an alternative route we should take for the first 8 km or so. After giving us all a childrens' sticker courtesy of the Seattle Police Department, he wishes us the best.

Over the Chehalis River, the new road brings us through dense forestry. Thick conifers line both sides of the road. Wide but gentle, the river doesn't have the power of the Yukon or the speed of the Skeena.

Gradually, we descend to the sea at Southbend, a town at the top of an inlet which proclaims itself to be 'The Oyster Capital of the World'. At the southern end of the town, we stop at a park, beside the bay. Neil prepares lunch as trawlers and speedboats enter and leave the bay. Seagulls perch on a nearby fence. New smells: seaweed, salt water and petrol fumes from outboard motors. After lunch, we cycle another 64 km down the road and arrive at the Pacific coastline of the United States.

4–7 August 2008

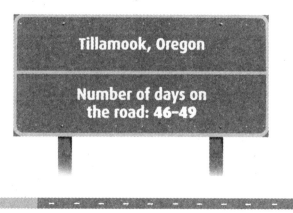

Tillamook, Oregon

Number of days on the road: 46–49

Number of kilometres completed: **4,352**

Washington and Oregon are famous destinations for cyclists and today is one of the best days of the journey yet. The weather is fantastic: a comfortable 30 °C with a lovely sea breeze keeping us cool. The road drops into bays and loops back up onto headlands. The ocean is a stone's throw away at all times. Often, the road runs close to the cliff's edge and, when it does, there are amazing views. Dozens of traffic lay-bys allow us to look out over the Pacific; sandy beaches hug the road south for as far as one can see. This highway will be our route for the next four weeks.

We haven't been able to stare into such a vast, undisturbed horizon for some time. The Pacific is the greatest ocean in the world. Its stillness, combined with its vastness, has a very calming, soothing effect and makes us feel we've been living in a harsh environment of trees and mountains up to now. This is a release from the tough environment of Alaska and Canada and the confusion of Vancouver and Seattle. Thousands of sea birds congregate on top of rocks covered in white guano.

The ocean always seems to present itself in the most dramatic fashion – rising in the distance gradually or appearing suddenly from around a corner. Over a wide inlet we cross from Washington to Oregon on Astoria Bridge. The region is famous for dairy produce and just outside the town there is a cheese factory, beside which we set up camp. Inside, dozens of people are queuing up for free cheese samples. There's even cheese ice cream. From a balcony on the top floor we can see the cheese being made. Later, we spend an hour on a pitch and putt course beside the factory.

Three other touring cyclists, who have been cycling down the coast, set up camp beside us: Gerard, Loren and Sarah. Gerard's plan is to tack east at some stage and eventually finish his trip in Florida. Gerard is an odd character in his late twenties with a beard down to his belly button; he wears children's clothes that don't fit him. He has hitch-hiked up here with his bike from LA to meet the two girls. The next morning, as we're getting ready to pull out, Gerard offers me some soil. He takes out a small tub from his pannier bag, removes the lid and guzzles down a mouthful of dry brown earth.

'Every morning, man. I've been doing it for six years now. That cereal you guys eat will kill you,' he says.

'Are you sure?'

'Yeah, man, it's one hundred per cent natural,' answers Gerard.

After another 120 km, we reach South Beach Provincial Campsite, which is packed full of holidaymakers from

Portland. The smell of burgers and hotdogs fills the evening air. Kids rush around on bikes and scooters. There's a far corner where we'll have enough room to camp. With our full entourage, our camp takes up a space about the size of a tennis court.

We sit around after dinner and shoot the breeze. Eric, who is cycling with us as far as San Francisco, is thinking out loud (as he often hilariously does) about how he could get away with murdering Gerard, the bloke we've just met. It quickly becomes a group discussion. We're all coming up with a fantasy like 'Death on the 101' and, as we're conjuring up the plot for the story, including the murder weapon and how we'd dispose of Gerard's body, Gerard and the two girls emerge from the darkness.

'Hey guys!'

An awkward silence descends as Gerard hangs his hammock up and the two girls pitch their tent. After five minutes, Gerard rolls over for a chat. The two girls follow him. One of the first things he tells us is his taste for breast milk.

'How did you get into that, Gerard?' I ask him.

'I used to work in KFC and one of the women who worked in the drive-through section had recently given birth, so I asked her for some of her milk. She said it would be all right, so I kept it in my fridge.'

Alan turns around and whispers to me, 'We're doing a hundred miles tomorrow to get rid of these muppets.'

8 August 2008

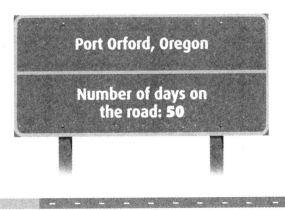

Number of kilometres completed: **4,626**

The coast of Oregon is even more spectacular than that of Washington, with mile after mile of undisturbed views of the ocean. The cycling is not hard when it is as beautiful as this.

Cycling south, everyone has a target, a city or place along the route they're aiming for. Over time, it becomes the same place for everyone, a collective goal. San Francisco seems to be our next target. We're talking about it the whole time, wondering what we'll do there, what we'll be able to see, the nightlife. San Francisco is where four of the group will leave us.

Without the countless hours of daylight we once had, we're making slower times. It gets dark at around 9 p.m. and, as we ride south, sunset is constantly getting earlier. Since we left Vancouver we haven't been making good progress and we're not hitting our daily targets. Ninety and hundred kilometre days are beginning to creep in to our routine.

75

We're not getting up early enough and not leaving early enough in the morning. It means we don't have a choice but to pull up short on our daily targets as the sun comes down every night. We're falling behind.

Continuing down the coast, we get stuck in an enormous traffic jam. It's not a problem because we can push on to the top but when we do so we are stopped by the police. There has been a major car accident. I can see the wreckage in the distance: twisted metal and scattered debris. The fire brigade, ambulances and the police are at the scene. Bodies are being put into ambulances and people are standing around with heads hung low and talking into mobile phones. I speak with the police officer at the top of the traffic jam and he says there has been a head-on collision. At least one person has died, he says.

This is the first time we've come across a human death on the road. The wreckage is eventually cleared and the traffic gets moving again but the thought of our own safety stays with me. What if one of us is hit by a car? What if one of us is killed? Time on the bike is often used to consider the hypothetical, an activity that rarely reaches a conclusion. But here is quite a rare moment when I conclude that if someone was in a serious traffic accident, the trip would come to an end and everyone would go home. Surely, if someone was knocked down, Alan, Kev, Brian and I would have to accept some of the responsibility? I cycle on and try and think of something else.

Our last stop in Oregon, before we pass into California, is the town of Port Orford. We're in Curry County. Not too far down the road is Cape Blanco. Apparently the weather will start to become much hotter from this point onwards but for the time being, the thick sea fog rolling in from the Pacific covers the entire village like a blanket. It's evening and the weather is much cooler. After a snack of fish and chips in a restaurant called The Crazy Norwegian, we cycle on another couple of kilometres to a campsite where we crash for the night. Dusk becomes night and a wall of fog hides the perfectly still ocean.

We have cycled 160 km today, as we said we would, which is satisfying. It's the type of day we have been in need of for a long time.

Eureka, California

Number of days on the road: 51–52

Number of kilometres completed: **4,900**

We cross into Crescent City, California. It's the beginning of what's going to be the most urbanised stretch of the journey. California is the third largest state in America and is about 1,200 km long, which means nine or ten cycling days. California's size and economic power make it one of the strongest self-contained regions, not only in America but in the world. In 2006, California's Gross Domestic Product was greater than all but eight countries in the world, even though, since then, things have gone a bit downhill.

California has, historically, laid claim to being different and independent. For many years, Alta California, the state we now know as California, remained a remote northern province of Mexico. In 1846, Alta rebelled against Mexican rule and proclaimed California a republic. The republic lasted for only twenty-five days, until the outbreak of the

Mexican–American War, when it capitulated to American forces who invaded from the bay of Monterey, a town we'll pass through in a few days. In January 1847, the Americans formally secured control of Alta California, which left the southern part of the region, Baja, still under the control of Mexico.

We cycle out of Crescent City to Eureka along the Redwood Highway, a road which, as its name suggests, weaves through the Californian Redwoods. The trees tower as much as 100 metres into the sky and their trunks measure up to 8 metres in diameter. Some are more than 2,000 years old.

The redwoods provide welcome shade. Their branches, high up in the canopy, shred the sunlight into hundreds of separate beams that dapple the road in front of us.

About thirty minutes after lunch I find myself on my own, cycling at a good pace. I reckon I'm about 90 km north of Eureka, so I decide to cycle on rather than waiting for the rest. The road hits the coast and then turns left, resuming a due south course. Big sand dunes between the beach and the road run south for kilometres.

As I approach Eureka, the only thing I can think of is that song by D. J. Mylo, the chorus of which is: 'So I took off on my bicycle and ended up in Eureka, California.'

But Eureka, California, is certainly not somewhere one would especially want to 'end up'. My impression is of a run-down town. At the first petrol station, I buy a few snacks and wait for the others. I don't know if anyone is out ahead of me or if I'm the farthest along. I haven't seen the support jeep yet, so I figure that Neil must be ahead, south of the town, like we agreed.

I cycle on through the town. It's not the California I had expected. Where are all the surfers and the blondes in bikinis? It's dark, dilapidated and the atmosphere is dead. A skinhead walks past with a pit-bull terrier, and a bloke wearing a singlet vest drives by me in an enormous pick-up truck. I stop at the southern end of the town beside Jake's Second Hand Gun Shop, just before the road turns back into highway.

An hour goes by and there's still no sign of anyone. Something has gone wrong or I'm lost. Dozens of scenarios of what might have happened come into my head. Am I on the right road? Did I take a wrong turn? Where is everyone else?

I cycle back into town, find a hotel and check my emails where I have saved Neil's mobile number. His voice at the other end is perfectly calm as usual.

'Neil, thank God, where are you? I've been cycling up and down this f***ing town for the past hour and a half.'

'Oh, hi, Ben, we're about 8 km north of Eureka in a campsite, we decided to pull up short,' says Neil.

I grit my teeth. 'OK grand, I'll see you in half an hour.'

Night has fallen. I'm furious. I cycle 8 km back up the road with no lights or reflectors on my bike. I curse out loud about everything that has been annoying me over the past couple of weeks. There is nothing worse than cycling back up the road.

Day 5 We leave the Arctic Circle, Alaska, *(l–r):* Alan Gray, John Garry, Ben, Brian McDermott, Kevin Hillier and Cillian O'Shea.

Day 33 Our sleeping arrangements aren't the most luxurious, *(l–r):* John Garry and Brian McDermott – the person on the left is either shy or in need of warmth!

Day 41 We cross Astoria Bridge from Washington to Oregon, *(l–r):* Kevin Hillier, Anthony Quinn and Mike Stewart.

Day 46 While cycling on the Interstate Highway 5, we get pulled over by a policeman who decides to go easy on us instead, *(l–r):* Anthony Quinn, Pat Anglim, Very Nice Policeman, Kevin Hillier, Tom Greaves, John Garry, Alan Gray, Mike Stewart and Eric Flanagan.

Day 55 This photo, taken in northern California, is my favourite, *(back row, l–r):* Anthony Quinn, Eric Flanagan, Brian McDermott, Ben, and Bryan Johnston; *(front row, l–r):* Killian Stafford, Mike Stewart, Neil McDermott, John Garry, Kevin Hillier, Alan Gray and Cillian O'Shea.

Day 74 Our first meeting with our FWG team in Tijuana, Mexico, *(l–r):* Ben, Anthony Quinn, Neil McDermott, Richard Boyd, John Garry, Tom Greaves, Lily, Cillian O'Shea, Alan Gray, Mickey, Rob Greene and Kevin Hillier.

Day 81 This is just one of the enormous cacti we encountered in Mexico, *(l–r):* Ben, Rob Greene, Alan Gray, Neil McDermott, Cillian O'Shea and Kevin Hillier.

Day 103 The coastline in Puerto Vallarta, Mexico, is a welcome sight.

Day 116 Antonio, one of our FWG escorts, gives an update to Brian McDermott at the Mexico–Guatemala border.

Day 126 Ben cycles with local children in Nicaragua.

Day 139 Cillian O'Shea, Ben (partially hidden) and Alan Gray battle the elements just over the Costa Rican border.

Day 169 Kevin Hillier and Cillian O'Shea lead the pack through the lowlands of Ecuador. Alan Gray, John Garry, Rob Greene and Ben follow behind.

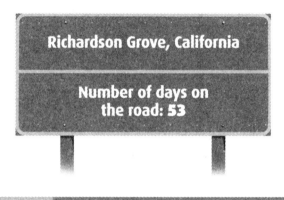

Number of kilometres completed: **5,000**

When I got into the campsite last night I was irritated, mostly at myself. It wasn't anyone else's fault I'd got lost. It had not been a good day all round. Eric and Tom had bad falls. Tom is fine but Eric's hip and leg are badly bruised. He won't be able to cycle for a couple of days.

We cycle through Eureka (the third time for me) and then inland, back among the giant redwoods. The temperature increases to 35 °C. The tourist attraction in this region centres on 'The legend of Bigfoot', an alleged ape-like creature purportedly inhabiting the forests around these parts. Bigfoot was named when a bulldozer-driver came across an enormous footprint in the forest, had it cast, photographed and printed in the *Humboldt Times*, the local rag, under the headline 'Bigfoot'. Scientists consider Bigfoot to be a combination of folklore and misidentification but despite this, Bigfoot, along with the Loch Ness monster, remains one of the most famous cryptids in the world. Amazingly, some people still come up here to try and find Bigfoot – actually try to track down this fictional beast. Unsurprisingly, the local economy takes full advantage and in gift shops along the road there are Bigfoot figures and t-shirts for sale.

We finish the day at Richardson Grove RV Park. In an evangelical church, set amongst the redwoods, I soon find myself having a conversation with the minister, Reverend Patrick Irwin. A fat, jolly character in his mid-fifties, his great-grandfather was from County Cork, he tells me. Reverend Irwin finishes sentences with phrases like 'The Lord works in mysterious ways' or with a quoted verse of the Bible. I tell him about our journey and say we'll be resting up in San Francisco for a few days when we arrive there. 'My home is only 16 km north of San Francisco and you would all be very welcome to camp in the garden if you like,' says Reverend Irwin.

'Thank you very much, Reverend, but we've already made plans.'

There's no polite way to tell this decent man that our plans include late nights, women and booze.

'A group of us get together to say prayers here every evening at 7 p.m., if you and your friends would like to come along,' says Reverend Irwin.

The church is at the centre of the campsite. Everyone we meet is very pleasant but there's something about the place that gives me the creeps, as if we're being judged from a distance. There's a shop on site which sells ice cream and cookies and each price label reminds the customer that the proceeds go towards 'the church'.

Day 54 It is amazing to see the size of the Californian Redwoods – here *(l–r):* Alan Gray, Tom Greaves and Mike Stewart pose with their bikes on the Redwood Highway.

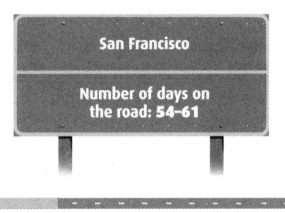

Number of kilometres completed: **5,388**

The signposts to San Francisco are becoming more frequent and the miles are quickly winding down. We cycle south, inland, through rolling country with steep, bare-topped hills surrounded by thick, scorched forestry. California becomes more like the Wild West I pictured as a child where cowboys and Indians fought it out high up in the hills, using cacti for cover.

On back roads we cycle towards San Francisco, up and over rolling hills with fields full of horses and down the Napa Valley, passing rows of vines protected from the road by tall conifers. Countryside changes into suburbia and suddenly there's the Golden Gate Bridge. It's covered in a heavy sea fog, so that all we can see of the world famous bridge are the tips of its gigantic red girders. Eric and I quickly realise that heavy traffic is coming against us as lights flash and horns blow furiously. We're trying to cycle the wrong way over the Golden Gate Bridge. We lift our bikes up over the side barrier and cycle into San Francisco, on the bridge's bike path.

Our first stop in San Francisco is a bar on Fisherman's Wharf where we toast our progress with a round of drinks. In the city centre, Brian and I attempt to cycle up Filbert Street, the steepest street in San Francisco.

'Get up, ya bastard!' I scream as I struggle up.

Five metres from the top, I come to a standstill and am forced to dismount. On our way towards the city's centre a homeless man is holding a sign which reads, 'Visions of a cheeseburger'. A noticeable amount of people are living on the streets; apparently, some by necessity and others by choice. On the corner of Post and Jones, right in the heart of the city near Union Square, we check into a hotel. Because a noisy construction site is right next door, we get a good deal. After we secure a holding room for the bikes and take a shower, we set out to explore the city.

We take taxis to an Irish pub on Haight Street, owned by a friend of John's father. Pints of Guinness and a slap up meal are presented to us, on the house. Haight Street is fantastic; the birthplace of the hippy movement in the 1960s. Haight Ashbury is awash with hippies and the homeless. Shops selling records and clothes line the streets. A culture of discussion and liberalism is still alive here; the area is full of people sitting around talking, exchanging ideas. As we wander towards the park at the end of Haight Street the smell of marijuana wafts though the evening air.

After a few days spent wandering around the town, dropping into cafés, observing this town with its fantastic laid-back atmosphere, it's clear to me that you'd have to do something extremely unusual to shock someone in San Francisco.

We've reached the end of the summer, the time where, in years gone by, we would all be going back to college. As Killian, Bryan, Eric and Tom return to their 'real' lives, there's a feeling for the first time that we, the people who aim to cycle to the end of this road, are not on a holiday. My mind goes back to the library in Trinity College where, in the spring of 2006, Alan Gray approached my desk and placed an enormous atlas in front of me. The open pages displayed the continents of North and South America. Alan told me that he wanted to cycle from top to bottom in nine months. I doubted the idea was possible. Too many problems, too many dangers, I thought – just too long. I'd never cycled more than a few kilometres in my life. Twenty-five thousand kilometres? No chance! I told Alan I thought it was a great idea, a once-in-a-lifetime adventure, but to count me out. After all, how would you even begin to organise a trip like that? How much training would you need to complete to consider taking it on?

Now, saying goodbye to the lads who are flying home, part of me envies them. Here we are, putting the spandex back on, pumping up our tyres and working out where we'll camp tonight. We're starting the journey again but this time more with a sense of duty. I know that if I don't reach the end of what I set out to do, I'll always be disappointed with myself. It doesn't really matter where you finish; it just matters that you arrive where you said you would. This is what keeps me going. Those of us who set out in Alaska won't be satisfied until we reach the end of the road.

20 August 2008

Santa Cruz, California

Number of days on
the road: **62**

Number of kilometres completed: **5,508**

On the first day after San Francisco, we come to Santa Cruz, which is located on the northern edge of Monterey Bay. We stop for lunch and try to work out the itinerary for the weeks ahead. It's mostly down to who's going to be coming and going but thankfully we're under no pressure to get to Los Angeles, our next major stop-off. Santa Cruz is the first really large-scale tourist resort we have encountered. A town of about 60,000 people, it's a world famous surfing destination. Dozens of volleyball courts line the beach in perfect rows, with funfairs and roller coasters stacked behind them. We stop at the end of a long pier and make sandwiches.

'San Fran is some city, isn't it lads?' says Cillian.

'How did we all fit into that hotel room?' I ask.

'No more booze for at least a week,' says Brian.

'A week? I'm never drinking again,' says John.

We continue south through vast fruit fields, and smell the sweet aroma of strawberries in the warm air. Hundreds of Mexicans are out in the fields, hunched over, picking the fruit. You can't see their faces, just their backs and covered heads as they pick the fruit, put it into boxes and then stack the boxes onto enormous trailers. Mexicans do a huge amount of the hard labouring in California.

A friend of Neil's, Richard Boyd, has flown out from Vancouver to join us. He's a funny, talkative lad and I can tell he'll be a fun addition to the group. 'Boyder' will ride in the car most days to keep Neil company but he does plan on cycling one of the spare bikes from time to time.

21 August 2008

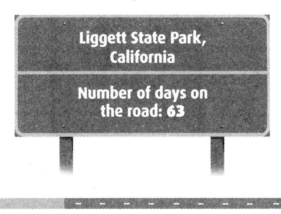

**Liggett State Park,
California**

**Number of days on
the road: 63**

Number of kilometres completed: **5,658**

We continue south through the flat agricultural region north
of Monterey and reach the town itself at noon.

Monterey is a seaside town with shops selling swimming
shorts, parasols and buckets and spades. It's also an
historical town; the capital city of California during its brief
period as a republic. We guzzle down sandwiches and take
off again. This region is expensive and the less time spent in
expensive resort towns, the better. We pass through the town
of Carmel, where we see palatial mansions with private
beaches that sweep down to the Pacific. We stop and take a
look at a group of four houses together, clustered in a small
cove and I'm told by a passer-by that the most modest of
them has a price tag of between four and six million dollars.
The houses look amazing, complete with private walkways
and swimming pools. Some are built into the natural

89

contours of the cliff and coast. The cycling is so much easier when the scenery is like this.

We arrive at Big Sur, a sparsely populated natural park where the Santa Lucia Mountains rise abruptly from the Pacific Ocean. 'The big south' or 'big country of the south', as it translates from Spanish, has the highest coastal peak of the Contiguous United States. Cone Peak, only 4 km from the ocean, is 1,571 metres above sea level. Few people live in this area owing to the high cost of real estate, tight planning laws and traditional local ways that try to protect the area's natural beauty.

We climb for about an hour and the road eventually evens out, presenting us with our most spectacular view yet of the Pacific. We're so high up, yet so near the ocean.

The group strings out and Kev and I find ourselves in front. We cycle side by side for another 8 km along the coast as the sun starts to sink over the Pacific, creating a spectacular mixture of red and orange light.

'Not a bad stretch of road, Benny?'

'Magic! Makes the years of organising worth the while, eh?'

Once Alan came up with the idea for the trip, Kev got involved immediately. Born in Kenya and schooled in Ireland, Kev's an all-rounder and a phenomenal organiser of people.

'Let's enjoy California. Something tells me things won't be as easy in Mexico,' he says.

We come across Neil at Liggett State Park Campsite, beside Sand Dollar beach. Kev, Tom and myself grab our shorts, cross the road and look for the nearest entrance to the beach to go for a swim. The beach is empty except for a couple who are sitting on distant rocks. The surf is big and the sea is mostly white. The moon shines a bright streak on the cold water. The icy fresh water cools and relaxes my legs.

Back at the campsite, we don't bother putting up the tents; we haven't been using them for some time now anyway. Instead, we just spread a tarpaulin underneath a big tree and sleep in the open air in our sleeping bags.

While lying down in the pitch dark, I see the outline of something moving in the tree above us.

'I think there's a squirrel or something in the tree, Brian,' I say.

'Hang on a sec till I get my torch. I think I see more than one.'

Brian shines the torch into the branches above us. Dozens of racoons cling to every branch of the tree and they stare down at us with their oversized eyes, swishing their thick bushy tails.

'Jesus Christ, they're like small dogs,' I say.

We move back a few metres so that we're not directly underneath them. It's harder to get to sleep knowing we're being watched from above.

22 August 2008

San Luis Obispo, California

Number of days on
the road: **64**

Number of kilometres completed: **5,688**

The racoons broke into the jeep last night. We left the front passenger window open. The little bastards ravaged their way through three boxes of breakfast cereal. You just can't leave food out at night. We adhered strictly to this rule in Alaska and Canada when there was a threat of bears – but racoons?

We get back on the road and pass by Elephant Seal Cove and then advance to our first break at Hearst Castle, the European-style castle designed for media tycoon Randolph Hearst and completed in 1947. The castle features prominently in Orson Welles' famous movie, *Citizen Kane*.

Myself and Cillian wander over to a café and have a bite to eat. Sometimes it's nice to take the day at your own pace, to operate within your own timetable rather than the group's. After lunch, we take the back roads between Route 1 and Route 101 through ranch and arable country. It seems we're properly into southern California. The landscape is sprinkled with palm trees and the temperature is definitely hotter. The road is beginning to present more classical examples of the California everyone has seen on television. We meet up with the others at Hot Springs Resort, just off Route 101, 160 km north of Santa Barbara. Hot spring baths are in front of the campsite and a thick stench of sulphur fills the air.

Alan, Kev, Brian and I have a meeting in the restaurant about what we need to tighten up on: better delegation and what the future might hold for the PACT brand.

'The mornings are a disaster, lads. We got into bad habits in Canada and we've never got out of them. Are we agreed that something has to be done?' I say.

'All well and good saying it, Benny, but we have to delegate properly. Everyone needs to start pulling their weight so we can get on to the road quicker,' says Alan.

'We need to talk about Mexico soon,' says Kev.

'Right, we're all agreed so; asses in gear in the mornings,' Brian says.

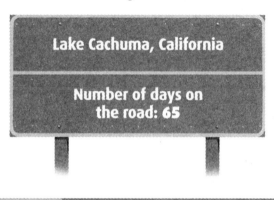

Lake Cachuma, California

Number of days on the road: 65

Number of kilometres completed: **5,823**

After all the talk, next morning comes and nothing changes. What's the point of discussing and agreeing that something is a problem if we're not going to try to improve it? We're not ready to move out for another half an hour, so I take the opportunity to ring home.

The reactions are very encouraging and make me feel proud. 'Well done', 'Good on ya' and 'Keep going' sound better coming from family members.

'How are you getting on?' I ask my brother, Will, whom I haven't spoken with for ages.

'Same old story, I'm in the office nine to five every week. A disaster!'

'Feels a bit like that here sometimes.'

'Enjoy it while you can. Not long till you'll be getting into the rat race yourself. Sounds amazing. Wish I could come out to you.'

It's great to be reminded about how well we're all doing but also to remember how lucky we are to be doing this.

About 30 km farther down the road, still north of Santa Barbara, we stop in Guadeloupe. The town is almost entirely inhabited by Mexicans and the architecture seems almost exclusively Mexican. We eat burritos and drink cold Coke from glass bottles. Mexico is not that far away now – a few hundred kilometres. Men wearing Stetsons, and with long moustaches, ride by on horseback.

A college mate of mine is spending the summer with some others in a town just north of Santa Barbara, called Isla Vista, another 80 km miles down the road.

When we eventually get to Isla Vista and meet up with the lads, it's great to see a few familiar faces. The town itself is almost completely made up of Irish students. Everyone is asking us about our trip. Many already know about our journey. Some are even talking about joining us.

Every night, it seems, there's a party on in one of the Irish houses, which have no furniture and are thick with rubbish and empty bottles. The doors are left open all the time and people come and go freely. Floods of Irish students throng the streets.

'So what do people do here during the day?' I ask a guy from Dublin whom I've just met.

'Ah nothing much. Sure, no one gets up until the afternoon anyway because we're out every night. Some people work a bit, I've gone surfing a few times but once you get out of bed, it's not long before you start pre-drinking for the night ahead again.'

The thought of spending three or four months here doing this is a world apart from our lives at the moment and I'm glad we're back on the bikes tomorrow.

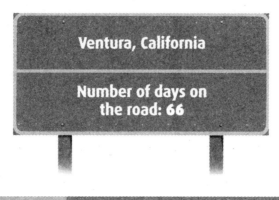

Ventura, California

Number of days on the road: 66

Number of kilometres completed: **5,908**

There was no need to set my alarm clock; I'm up and ready to go by 0845.

The approach roads to Santa Barbara are brutally steep; long, drawn-out climbs in the hot sun. And it is really hot now. After about 8 km, we spot a turn-off signposted 'bike detour'. There's no traffic. We climb to a small restaurant and bar called 'Cold Springs Tavern'. Rows of Harley Davidsons are parked up outside, a huge collection of chrome gleaming in the bright sun. Dozens of bikers in their leathers are sitting outside drinking beer. Some have outrageous beards and most have devil or skull-and-cross-bone tattoos.

'Why you guys gotta make us look so lazy?' one shouts over to us.

They appear terrifying but they couldn't be any cooler.

There's a band outside the tavern playing Blue Grass. The music is pumping and the beer is flowing but, as always, we have to get back on the road.

Santa Barbara is very wealthy and very clean, full of expensive cars and beautiful women. We're unshaven, dirty and sticking out like sore thumbs. I see a lovely blonde sitting outside a café. She's gorgeous. She stares back at me. Then I cycle into the back of Kevin's bike and go flying over the handlebars. I scramble to my feet, trying not to embarrass myself too much.

Pedestrians start clapping.

'Hey, nice recovery, man!'

The blonde gets to her feet and walks off, smiling.

Leaving the bikes at the Ventura RV Park, beside the freeway, we walk into Ventura to meet Neil and Brian's dad, Niall, who has flown out from Dublin.

Inevitably, we get on to the topic of what's going on at home.

'It's going down the tubes, lads. It'll be a different country when you get home.'

We'd heard things were bad, but not that bad.

'Bank shares are tanking and the arse is falling out of the property market,' says Niall. 'You're better off here at the moment. Country's going to be wiped out.'

Santa Monica, California

Number of days on
the road: **67**

Number of kilometres completed: **5,995**

We cycle out of Ventura and stop at a bike shop to buy tubes and a few other items. Back on Highway 1, right by the coast, we see a body bag being put into an ambulance. Is that a dead person? we ask each other.

'Just saw them zip it up,' says John.

Malibu, Hollywood's home of rich and famous, is one of the least impressive places I've come across on the trip. Why, I wonder, if you were a multimillionaire, would you chose to live here? The coast is obstructed from the road by a continuous row of houses. I look back at the hills overlooking the town and every inch is crammed with houses, each one more extravagant than the other. The sides of the road are chock-a-block with Porsches, Ferraris and Rolls-Royces.

'Don't know what all the fuss is about?' I say to Alan as we cycle through.

He agrees.

On the outskirts of Santa Monica, we meet Neil and Niall, who have checked everyone into the 'Hotel California'. We drink a few beers at a bar opposite the hotel and, after we shower, Niall takes us out to an Italian restaurant for dinner. This means a lot. We need these types of rewards every now and again. After the meal, Alan, Kev and I go back to the hotel and the rest walk across to a Mexican bar for margaritas.

The three of us sit up for a couple of hours, have a few smokes and chat about how things are going.

'We're spending too much money. We haven't cycled a third of the trip and I've spent half my budget,' Alan says.

'I'm in the same boat. At this rate, we'll be eating from cans of sardines by the time we get to Peru,' says Kev.

'What about safety, lads? Should we not insist that everyone wears helmets?' I ask.

Since the start of the trip, the use of helmets has been lax. Some are wearing them now and again, others never. The body bag in Ventura is fresh in my mind.

It turns out Alan has been worrying about the same thing. We all agree to use San Diego as the point to implement change. It's not far away now. This trip will change dramatically after that.

26 August 2008

Hermosa Beach, Los Angeles,
California

Number of days on
the road: **68**

Number of kilometres completed: **6,020**

We have breakfast with the owner of Hotel California, Rik, who said he'd pay for it, but we end up paying for it ourselves. Rik is a huge man with a mane of blond-grey hair and a matching goatie beard. His father was from Skerries in Dublin but emigrated to Newfoundland in the 1940s. Rik owns a chain of hotels, he says, in San Francisco and in Newfoundland and they're all called 'Hotel California'. Although he says he owns all these hotels and the patent for the name 'Hotel California', after his promise to buy breakfast, I don't really believe him.

We don't hang around. By cycling along the beaches we're able to avoid traffic. The sand, white and perfectly clean, looks almost man-made. The people on the volleyball courts fit the same description: bleached blonde hair and excessively worked out bodies.

We cycle as far as Venice Beach. The street is full of cheap t-shirt shops and people out on the streets advertising medicinal marijuana for sale, as it is legal in this part of the country for certain medical conditions. Cheap electronic stores and pawnshops and casual vendors are everywhere. At the famous Venice Beach Gym, pictures of champion bodybuilders line the walls. We have some noodles in a small Chinese takeaway, then walk with the bikes for a while because there are just too many people about. Lifeguard stations and long piers stick out into the Pacific. We walk as far as Hermosa Beach where we take a few hotel rooms.

San Diego, California

Number of days on
the road: **70**

Number of kilometres completed: **6,160**

After cycling through Huntington, Laguna and Newport Beaches, I think it's safe to assume we're out of LA. What you don't see in the movies or on television shows are the enormous factories and oil refineries which lie just behind these beaches. Much of the oil being processed in LA comes from Prudhoe Bay, Alaska, where we began our trip ten weeks ago.

We'll be in San Diego tonight. Niall's brief stint with the group is over; he has to get back to Ireland. We all leave early and arrange to rendezvous with the support team in San Diego. Niall will be crossing paths with Rob Greene, another friend from college who is coming out to finish the rest of the trip with us.

Through a series of back roads, we cycle past a US army base where tanks are out practising war games, weaving through man-made mounds, targets and other obstacles. Apparently it's possible to take a detour through the military area instead of getting back on the interstate. At the entrance we ask the two soldiers stationed there whether we can pass through. They don't think it's possible because we're not US nationals, a fact they confirm with a quick phone call.

'So you fellas have come from Alaska. Holy s***, how are your asses?' says Ramirez, the smaller of the two soldiers. 'That's an awesome effort. Enjoy San Diego. With those accents you'll clean up!'

Now we're back on Interstate 5 again for the first time since coming out of Seattle. I'm reminded how much I hate the fast dangerous traffic. At lunch, at a state beach 24 km north of San Diego, I get back into the jeep to have a rest. The radio station has cut to a commercial break. The first ad, for a car dealer, goes like: 'In a celebrity driven world it's all about who you know and what you drive.'

I burst out laughing. Southern California in a nutshell.

Tom has arranged for us to stay with an old family friend in San Diego. As a kid, he used to spend time in a resort in Canada where he met a tennis professional called Trip Gordon. Trip now lives in Coronado in San Diego and said to Tom that he'd be delighted to have us all over to stay. It'll be a good call on our first night in the city.

Coronado is an island off San Diego which has been connected to the mainland and the downtown area of the city by a bridge since only 1969. The houses here are the most expensive in San Diego. Since no cyclists are allowed on the bridge, we make the short ferry journey to the island. Coronado is immaculate. Houses have white picket fences and pristinely kept gardens. A golf course weaves around some of the residences.

It's hard to think Trip Gordon was ever a professional tennis player. He's about five feet five, has a giant pot belly and a bright red face. Kelly, his wife, is about six feet tall with long brown hair and great legs; she used to be a model. Their son, Henry, is about nine or ten years old.

'I've been expecting you s*** stains. I got two kegs tapped. You guys are Irish, right?' says Trip.

I can tell we're going to like this guy.

Before we get stuck in for the night, Alan and I go to the airport and collect Rob who has brought out some things we requested from home: bars of Cadbury's chocolate and bottles of Buckfast, a fortified wine that we drank during college days. Rob is excited to get going on the bike. I love the energy any newcomers bring with them.

In Trip's house things look like they're starting to take off.

'Where have you f***ers been? These other s*** stains have nearly finished the keg,' says Trip.

Trip is behind the keg pouring pints and Kelly is running around the place making sure everyone has enough to eat. It's not long before the bottles of Buckfast are produced and a proper party kicks off. Trip is having a great time. His stepson AJ and AJ's friend Horton come over and get stuck in. They're burly tall men in their thirties, ex-American football players.

'You Irish think you can drink? Let's DRINK!'

Trip moves on to vodka and tonics and it's not long before everyone is very drunk.

'What the hell is going on here? Who is this maniac?' Rob asks.

'He's a friend of Tom's. Just met him; we're camping in his garden tonight,' I tell him.

Trip decides we'll go into the village of Coronado and find a bar. We walk out the front gate and when I look back I see him cycling a beach cruiser down his driveway with his trousers around his ankles!

'Out of my way, s*** stains!'

He veers off to the side of the path and crashes into the hedge. A couple of the lads help him to his feet and we all walk up the street, arm in arm, singing.

With the hangover the next day comes the cold wind of reality. Trip, Kelly and Henry head off to San Francisco for a few days' holidays but insist we're welcome to stay on in their house. The cycling trip as we have known it for the past two months is just about to change: we'll cycle out of comfortable San Diego and into Mexico. We'll have to deal with the language barrier, change of diet, tighter security and infrequent services. The next 16,000 km will take us down some of the poorest, most underdeveloped and dangerous roads in the world.

I'm looking forward to the new challenge. In order to remain interesting the trip needs to change or the daily routine would become dull and the trip itself difficult to endure. When one cycles every day, the physical demands recede, so alternative environments and different sceneries are needed for enthusiasm to remain high. Cycling for cycling's sake is not enough.

The change at the American–Mexican border will be immediate and is often referred to as the starkest change of environment in the world.

A meeting in Trip and Kelly's living room is convened and we make it clear to everyone that, in many ways, the party is over. We're going to have to be far more conscious of security and our own personal safety. Only a few of us have some basic Spanish. We won't be able to explain easily to local people what we're doing. We won't be able to endear ourselves easily to people. The police have an awful reputation in Mexico and bribery will be something that we will have to be aware of and possibly engage in. I raise the topic of helmets and say, that for the record, we are advising everyone to wear one. Alan talks about expenditure and how we'll have to start cutting back. Kev talks about looking after your own gear and bikes.

They're all good points but the main emphasis of the meeting is to remind everyone that we're just about to cycle into the Baja desert, so 'let's get our mind set right, lads'. We can only plan for what we know and what we have researched, yet the truth is we don't know much about Mexico. What we do know is that we'll be cycling through it for the next seven weeks.

MEXICO

31 August 2008

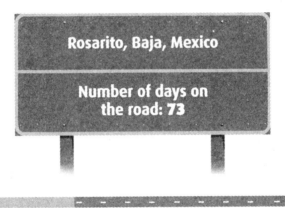

Rosarito, Baja, Mexico

Number of days on
the road: **73**

Number of kilometres completed: **6,224**

Before we left Ireland, Brian arranged for a security detail to accompany us through Mexico and Central America for our safety. The security company, called Freight Watch Group or FWG, was founded seven years ago by a cousin of Brian's, an ex-Irish Army officer, Kieran O'Connor. FWG follows cargoes of expensive goods being transported along the dangerous Mexican highways. The private security business is thriving in Mexico, since state authority and police can't be relied upon for adequate protection against hijacking by highway gangs and drugs cartels.

We're scheduled to meet representatives of FWG today in Tijuana, just over the US border. We cleaned up Trip's house before we took off and, for fun, posed for a group photo of us all dressed up in Trip's clothes – jackets, caps and shirts – beside a sculpture of a horse that's in his back garden. We arrange to have the picture framed and hang it on his living room wall, ready for him to see when he returns home from San Francisco.

South of Coronado, we pass a large army training assault course. As we approach Tijuana, border control vans roam the streets. An enormous red sign reads MEXICO. We cycle past the sign without producing a passport or giving anyone a reason why we're here.

FWG are meant to meet us in a car park beside the border offices. We look back to see American officials checking cars, conducting searches and inspecting documents of the large crowd waiting patiently to go north. A Mexican official barely takes a second look at me as he lounges back in his chair.

We sit tight for an hour, then two men and a young woman pull up in an 'FWG' jeep. They seem very pleased to see us and give each of us a giant sombrero. The girl, the only member of the three who speaks English, is called Lily. She's twenty-one years of age, has long, black, curly hair and the kind of figure that touring cyclists can only dream of. She'll be with us for the day only. The two men will be escorting us as far as La Paz, the town at the very end of the Baja peninsula, Lily says. They're short squat guys from Mexico City and look as hard as coffin nails. One of them, Mellie, is in his mid-forties, unshaven, with a gold tooth, and he chain smokes. No one can grasp the other man's name, so we call him Mickey, because his t-shirt has a picture of Mickey Mouse on it. Mickey is of similar age to

Mellie, although slightly more groomed. He wears a thick gold chain around his neck.

FWG want us to spend the night in Tijuana but we insist on pushing on while it's still light enough to do so. We've heard awful things about Tijuana and none of us fancies spending the night here. So we follow their jeep out of town.

Leaving Tijuana, the contrast with San Diego unveils itself. Along the sides of the streets children and dogs play in mounds of rubbish. People are crammed into the most destitute looking dwellings. This is where American students come to drink cheap tequila. If I referred to our time in the US as the expedition's vacation, that vacation has ended abruptly.

Our destination for the night is Rosarito, a town about 50 km south of Tijuana. FWG are unsure of the route, so we spend a lot of time back-tracking and going in wrong directions as FWG constantly change their minds. There is a long steep climb coming out of Tijuana. The group is pushing it much harder than usual in an effort to get a better look at Lily, who is standing out of the sun roof of the FWG jeep in front, taking pictures of us as we push hard up the hill. After an hour we find the right road. Half a dozen freshly killed dogs lie with their entrails exposed in the afternoon sun. The smell fills the air. We pass taco bars. People turn their heads to watch us spin by. Children wander around on the side of the road and shout after us.

By 8 p.m. we arrive at Rosarito and check into a hotel called Puepito. Rosarito, on the coast, is dominated by flashing neon lights, bars, clubs and strip clubs, all of which stay open all night. FWG drive off to find a hotel for themselves. We agree to meet them at our hotel at nine in the morning. Lily takes off back to Mexico City and says she'll see us farther down the coast. We stroll down the town to look for something to eat. Myself, Brian, Cillian and Kev sit at the counter of a taqueria – a taco bar – and order some burritos and quesadillas.

Later, while I lie in bed, my mind is focused on the desert ahead.

1 September 2008

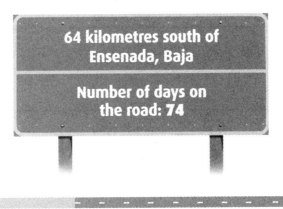

64 kilometres south of Ensenada, Baja

Number of days on the road: 74

Number of kilometres completed: **6,372**

Another month has clocked up. Today's the real beginning of the Baja peninsula, the portion of Mexico that juts out from the United States. The South Pacific lies to the west and the Sea of Cortez to the east.

Looking at the map, you would be forgiven for thinking the peninsula isn't very long but, measuring almost 1,800 km, Baja is the longest peninsula in the world.

It's strange cycling with the security detail driving at a snail's pace directly behind us. Baja has traditionally been a notoriously dangerous province of Mexico, with high levels of violent crime, murder and drug-trafficking. Although these days it's a great deal safer, Mexico is still a world leader in abduction and kidnapping. The drug gangs and cartels, operating mostly along the northern border in such cities as Tijuana and Juarez, are highly organised and violent, regularly carrying out 'hits' on the police and government officials. The police themselves are notoriously corrupt and are thought to be as much a part of the problem as the criminals, accepting bribes and ensuring the freedom of trafficking throughout the country's checkpoints. The army, considered to be the 'good guys' in this enduring affair, are now very visible in the province and there are regular army checkpoints along the road.

We cycle into the barren, scorched Baja Desert, leaving behind the urbanised border sprawl. Thousands of toweringly tall cacti and boulders as big as houses are visible all the way to the horizon. The heat becomes more intense and makes cycling most uncomfortable. I bucket sweat, which quickly evaporates, leaving a salty residue on my skin. The salt stains my black cycling gear, creating white patterns that everyone in the group finds hilarious. No one else sweats quite as much as I do.

We have lunch outside a hotel at the northern outskirts of Ensenada. The usual menu of sliced-pan sandwiches is now a thing of the past and has been replaced by cornflour tortillas and soft, tasteless Mexican cheese. It seems to me that all Mexican food is a variation of the same ingredients: tortillas, *carne* (meat), *queso* (cheese), salsa (sauce), rice and beans. These ingredients go into the making of burritos, quesadillas, enchiladas, tacos and most other dishes.

The language barrier is already causing us problems. 'Which route should we take out of the town?', 'will there be anywhere suitable to camp 50 km south?', 'will there be any services in the town?' are questions we are semi-capable of asking in Spanish, but the answers don't make much sense to us. Using Mellie and Mickey, and with a lot pointing and gesturing, we eventually learn that there is a campsite at a resort 70 km south of Ensenada. We aim to get there about four hours after lunch.

Young Mexican couples hang out by the campsite's swimming pool. It's more expensive than any of us had expected but has a very well stocked shop and a tap, with as much running water as we want. It is Anthony and Tom's last night before they return home, so the gang will be cut back to a smaller group of eight by the time we get deeper into Baja.

The FWG vehicle that trails us has a large sign warning drivers that there are cyclists ahead – a necessary precaution on these busy and sometimes dangerous roads.

Odette, Baja

Number of days on
the road: **75**

Number of kilometres completed: **6,500**

Before we leave the campsite, we give the lads who are going home a big hug and say we'll see them next March in Dublin. It seems like an eternity away. Neil is driving them back to San Diego; we agree to see him on the road after lunch.

We don't normally cycle in a bunch, rather in ones and twos, with distances of a couple of hundred metres opening up between everyone. This is not predetermined but just seems to have evolved. Mellie and Mickey, driving behind in the jeep, stop us midway through the morning and gesture to us that they'd prefer if we stayed together in a bunched up group rather than strung out like we are.

'*Compacto, por favor,*' Mellie says.

It seems hostage gangs might take advantage of a strung out group so, from then on, we cycle in a tight group, just in front of the jeep.

Our first break is at a small shop just north of San Vincente, where we eat more soft, tasteless cheese wrapped in tortillas. Everyone thinks it's so vile that we take another break, 10 km farther down the road, at a restaurant with a western menu and an outdoor seating area on shaded veranda. It's far hotter now than ever. Each of us guzzles back two or three bottles of water. The scorched desert terrain is relieved occasionally by plantations of vines and wheat. With the permission of a local farmer we set up camp in a field that is surrounded by rusting farm machinery: old tractors, ploughs and trailers. Neil sets up the camping cooker on the back of a hay trailer and prepares a meal. Alan, ever the farmer, having grown up on a dairy farm in Kildare, inspects the farm machinery.

We fill up a camping shower, hang it from the corner of an old washing line and take turns. Just before dinner, Miguel, the farmer comes out, asks us if everything is OK and presents us with some fresh drinking water. A tall thin man in his sixties, he seems to be living alone. The sun begins to set behind the scorched hills, lighting up the countryside in a deep glowing orange. The desert glows as the day slips away.

Number of kilometres completed: **6,631**

Alan is feeling sick, having not slept much last night, so we delay departure by an hour. We didn't put up the tents last night but slept in the open. The temperature drops quickly here as the night goes on so Alan may have caught a chill. Unless one of us becomes so ill that we can't continue, our policy is that the group will carry on. This is the unwritten rule; in order for cycling to stop, someone's illness has to be very serious but Alan's ready to roll within an hour of taking on some food and water.

We cycle 32 km in just over an hour, about as quick as it gets. After a short break, it's a slightly slower 40 km to the town of San Quentin where we have lunch. There's a street market on the side of the road, across from a school, selling fruit and vegetables. Kids are on their break, playing football but most of them are at the playground fence, motionless, staring at these strange and pasty cyclists who have just arrived in their town.

It's not as hot as yesterday: there's a haze and a breeze coming from the west. We take a quick stop for water 35 km later and then hit a very long and energy sapping uphill slog before dropping rapidly into El Rosario. Situated on the bend of the road and just before the high desert plateau, El Rosario is small with only a handful of services. The streets are clean and hanging baskets full of red flowers brighten the fronts of houses. We get permission to pitch the tents at the back of a hotel at the northern entrance to the town. Everyone heads off to bed at about 9 p.m. but I sit up and read. When I get into my sleeping bag I feel a familiar stinging bite on my arm: mosquitoes. It has been nine weeks since I've felt this particular discomfort. Noise comes from the road and the outside lights of the hotel remain on all night.

4 September 2008

Rancho Santa Ynes, Baja

Number of days on the road: 77

Number of kilometres completed: **6,761**

Six o'clock and our earliest ever start! I love getting on the road early. On our way on to the desert plateau, we stop to stock up on water, biscuits and cigarettes for the short breaks we'll have throughout the day. It takes half an hour to climb to the desert plateau but since it's the morning and not so hot, the cycling is not too hard on the legs. Rocks and boulders covered in bright graffiti are sprinkled in between the cacti.

Signposts indicate towns that are 50 km off the road, in the middle of the desert. You could find yourself deep and lost in the Mexican desert in no time. The place where we planned to have lunch turns out not to have any services and the village on the map doesn't exist. The map can no longer be trusted. Two further roadside restaurants are closed down.

After another 20 km we arrive at yet another 'restaurant' which appears to have been closed for some time.

We're hungry, we're all out of water. We dismount and take shelter from the unrelenting midday sun. At 42 °C, it's the hottest I have ever experienced. On the bike there's nowhere to hide from the sun. It beats down on top of you relentlessly, burning you, drying you out and sapping your energy.

We urgently need to find water and food. Another 30 km is covered in the searing heat. My throat dries out and I begin to feel faint. All remaining water is shaken out of bottles. The pace of cycling drops hugely.

'Something needs to happen, we need water, I reckon another half hour, tops, before one of us can't go on,' Alan says.

After another 5 km, around an enormous desert mound, a roadside shop and restaurant appear. The path leading to it is lined with the skulls of dead animals. Rob, who's still getting used to the daily demands, is dehydrated and a big concern. He lies down on the restaurant floor as we bring him a selection of drinks. We all drink two litres of fluids each. The drinks are kept in huge ice coolers in the kitchen. These roadside shacks have no electricity or running water.

I lie down on the cold tiles and fall asleep, my drenched body staining the floor. It takes about two and a half hours for us to get back into any condition to resume progress. The restaurant owner lets us be, happy with the business we're giving them.

Some 25 km later we cycle through a part of the road that, amazingly, is flooded. The water comes up to our calves and after a few minutes our legs are drenched. Luckily, it takes only a few minutes for everything to be bone dry again.

At 6 p.m. we reach Cataviña and set up camp at Rancho Santa Ynes. The campsite is a tract of cleared land adjacent to an old farm building owned by a family. Having pitched the tents we head over to the house for tacos that a sign at the entrance maintains are the best in Baja. For $6 each we get two tacos, an enchilada and a soda; not the great value I had expected. I imagine we'll have to get farther away from the US before real Mexican prices emerge. It's pitch dark and we return to the tents. The sky is full of stars. I decide to sleep outside and it's like being inside a giant sparkling dome. As I doze off a coyote howls in the distance: it's my first time hearing this sound.

5 September 2008

Punta Prieta, Baja

Number of days on the road: 78

Number of kilometres completed: **6,878**

As much cycling as possible needs to be done before the hottest part of the day. Ideally, we should be getting the majority of the cycling done before lunchtime, at which point we can take a big break and avoid the unbearable heat. The rest of the day can then be finished out in the late afternoon.

At 10.30 a.m., after 50 km, we arrive at a roadside restaurant. Beyond this point, there's nothing else but desert for 80 km, or so the map says. This restaurant is the most basic we have come across yet. Faded jigsaw puzzles along with portraits of the Virgin Mary decorate the walls. The lino on the floor is worn and torn off in places. There are half a dozen small tables with four wooden chairs at each. We are the only customers. An old lady, hunched as she shuffles around the restaurant floor, says she'll prepare some food. There is no menu. A plate of three narrow burritos, salsa and quesadillas are presented after fifteen minutes. You eat what you get or you go hungry.

Today is hotter than yesterday. I walk outside to the support jeep where the thermometer reads 112 °F; 45 °C. As the clock ticks to 3 p.m. and it remains just as hot as before, we take off.

When we get to Punta Prieta, our destination for the day, most of us are dehydrated. My neck and legs are badly burnt; I haven't been that diligent in applying sunscreen. After discovering that there are no camping sites or hotels available, we ask a local shopkeeper if we can camp behind his shop. His back yard is covered with old bangers, farm machinery, barrels, crates and other clutter. We set about putting up the tents.

Finding a barrel of rainwater in the corner of the yard I use a cup and rinse myself down, making sure to clean all the salt off my body.

6 September 2008

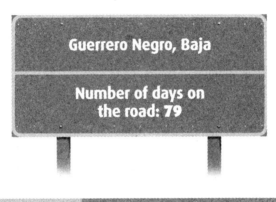

Guerrero Negro, Baja

Number of days on the road: 79

Number of kilometres completed: **7,000**

I'm up at 5.40 a.m. and first out of the tent.

'Good morning, guys! It's another beautiful day in the desert!'

'What time is it, you maniac? Get back in here!' John shouts.

Reluctantly, people start getting up.

Guerrero Negro marks the midpoint of the Baja peninsula. Progress in Mexico has been fast, despite the heat. Possibly as fit as we have ever been, we're all still in good shape, although fitness on the bike seems to ebb and flow. We can go a week where we're sluggish and then the following week everyone will be full of energy.

Mellie says there may be a passport check on the road approaching Guerrero Negro but it proves to be a false alarm and as we enter the town we're waved through by the military.

Our presence in Mexico is still officially unaccounted for. We do actually wish to register the fact that we're here because we don't want to breach the terms of our US visas. To all intents and purposes we are still in the United States of America because we were never stamped out crossing the border. At about 2 p.m., we arrive at Guerrero Negro. The town comprises one long street of taco bars and shops selling cheap clothes and other touristy merchandise. Whale watching is the main attraction here. The watching season runs from December to April, so now the town is quiet.

After we check into Baja Mision Hotel, I spend the afternoon sleeping. At 7 p.m., we go out for beers and fish tacos.

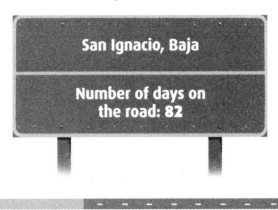

San Ignacio, Baja

Number of days on
the road: 82

Number of kilometres completed: **7,150**

Before taking off, we stock up with bottled water and minerals. The road south is perfectly flat. Contrary to what the map indicates, all the settlements we come across are abandoned or don't exist. There's nowhere to stop for lunch so we cover almost 100 km on empty stomachs. Then we stop at the side of the road for a short break. Cacti tower above us on both sides.

Finishing whatever biscuits and snacks we have, we continue for another 40 km, arriving at San Ignacio, our stop-off point for the night. San Ignacio has both an old and a new town; we set up at a campsite which lies just off the road between the two.

I stroll into the Spanish colonial old town, situated around a square with a church at its northern end. The village, located in an oasis, is sheltered from the sun by a canopy of broad-leafed trees in the centre of the square. It is so cool here compared to the desert and there is a sense of peace. Walking towards the church, I hear a chorus of women's voices. Popping my head inside the building, I instantly feel the deeper cool. Having just finished up, the ladies walk out of the church against me, each in turn saying hello. While sitting here, it is hard to imagine the fiery battle ground of the desert which we have come from and which continues up ahead.

9–10 September 2008

Loreto, Baja

Number of days on
the road: 82–83

Number of kilometres completed: **7,422**

We climb out of the oasis of San Ignacio, the lowest point of the desert, close to the aquifer. Our destination is the Sea of Cortez, on the eastern side of the peninsula. Our heading is due east, towards an enormous volcano called Tres Viregenes. The quality of the land and the soil on both sides of the road has improved and now seems capable of sustaining growth. Neil catches up with us in the support jeep after 50 km and with him are three of his friends who are going to keep him company for a few weeks. We pull over in the shadow of the volcano and meet the new arrivals: Jenny, Andrew and Paul.

'Welcome to the Pan American Cycle Test, guys. Strap yourselves in,' says Alan.

'It's not cycle-cycle-cycle the whole time, lads, is it?' asks Paul.

'When we're not cycling, we're either sleeping, eating or drinking. Simple stuff really,' Cillian replies.

After we pass the volcano we head towards Santa Rosalia. Cycling over the volcano we get the best views of the desert yet: sand, cacti and rocks for as far as the eye can see. Cycling down we get our first views of the Sea of Cortez, glistening like millions of diamonds.

Then 20 km after we hit the coast, we arrive at Santa Rosalia. It's an old-fashioned Mexican fishing town and, like San Ignacio, it is based around a large square. We arrive as the local school are on their lunch break. Dozens of children run about in a playground adjacent to the restaurant where we're having lunch. I lie down for ten minutes in the main square before we get going again. At 5 p.m., we arrive at Isabel RV park about 2 km outside of Mulegé.

'So this is The Unbelievable Trip. How does it feel to be so far into it?' asks Jenny after I pitch the tents.

Jenny is the first female member of the team and brings a civilising influence to conversation and behaviour generally.

'I'm fairly wrecked,' I say. 'How long are you all staying for?'

'We'll see. Probably until some time in Central America. How long will it take you to get to Panama?'

'If we keep motoring like we are, fingers crossed, by early or mid-November.'

In the morning the views from the road are spectacular; it's overcast and the coastal mountain range is a deep shade of blue, a *Lord-of-the-Rings* type vista but with a distinctly Mexican feel. For thirty minutes it pours, the first indications of the impending rainy season. It keeps pouring.

The road quickly turns into a cascading river. Rocks and lumps of mud are washed on to the road.

At 9 p.m., as we wait in the car park of a hotel, it rains biblically. Rain water gushes through the roof tiles of the gazebo we intended to sleep in. It's too late and wet to pitch tents. I take my sleeping bag and wander over to an open garage at the side of the hotel. Finally out of the rain, I slide underneath a pick-up truck where I doze off.

11 September 2008

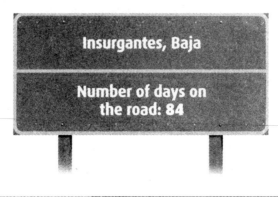

Number of kilometres completed: **7,567**

I slide out from underneath the truck and look around me.
The rest of the group are in the garage too, underneath
tables, trailers and cars.

'Well, that's a first. I'll probably never sleep under a
speedboat again,' Cillian says.

For the first few kilometres, mutterings within the group
arise that we might not be able to camp out too regularly if
it's too wet. Jenny sits in the FWG car for the morning and
takes pictures of our last days in Baja. The countryside
becomes greener and, for a couple of kilometres, the road is
completely covered with tiny frogs the size of your thumbnail.
Not all of them make it. For two kilometres, progress is
accompanied by a constant crushing noise as an enormous
massacre of frogs takes place. The constant loud clicking
noise coming from the vegetation on both sides of the road

is cicadas, a type of insect, according to Mellie. The land is productive and there are vast fields of corn and wheat. We reach the town of Insurgentes. From here it's 210 km to La Paz, where we'll get the ferry across the Sea of Cortez to Mazatlán in mainland Mexico.

'Let's get it all done today, lads. Big night out in La Paz tonight. Sound good to everyone?' says Brian.

'Sounds like a fantastic plan. Think I might have to cycle in with you!' says Paul.

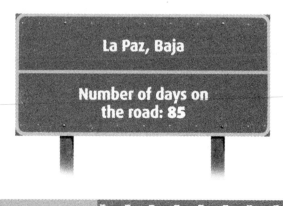

La Paz, Baja

Number of days on
the road: **85**

Number of kilometres completed: **7,777**

Brian takes a spare bike out of the trailer and gets Paul set up; he's never cycled more than a few kilometres before. We take lunch after 100 km at a little shack of a restaurant. The owners are delighted to see us and when we arrive, two squat women immediately start cooking meat and warming up tortillas on a hot plate. They pile the tortillas on to a breadboard and cover them with a tea towel to keep them warm. Saucers of salsa and cold bottles of Coca-Cola are brought out. The room is full of plants and jars of insects are displayed on shelves. One jar contains an enormous tarantula and there's a tank with a snake in the corner of the room.

We guzzle back the tacos and, not wanting to waste too much time, get back on the road, which is totally flat for the next 30 km. I listen to my iPod, where Christy Moore sings,

'Oh Lisdoonvarna, Lisdoon, Lisdoon, Lisdoon, Lisdoonvarna!'

I feel in really good shape. Eventually, I turn around and see that the rest of the group isn't behind. For another 15 km I press on and eventually come to the top of a steep hill where I dismount to wait for everyone. From the brow of the hill I see La Paz in the distance, 40 or 50 km away. I wander over to a building at the side of the road and have a look around for water. A small dog barks furiously from behind the closed front door. No one is at home. At the back of the house I find a large blue barrel covered with a sheet of plywood. Beautiful, beautiful water. Thinking back to all the advice we got in Ireland about dirty, unpurified water and how it 'would make you sick beyond belief', I smile. I scoop the water into the bottles, take an enormous gulp and pour the remainder of the contents over my head. After another fifteen minutes, the group is back together again and we cycle quickly downhill to the coast, to La Paz and the end of Baja peninsula.

Paul is delighted with himself.

'And you've all been cycling for months!' he shouts to us, as he hurtles rapidly downhill.

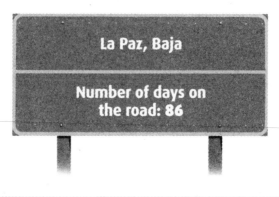

La Paz, Baja

Number of days on the road: 86

Number of kilometres completed: **7,777**

A sore thumping in my head is the first sign of a day-long hangover. Too many tequilas last night and we have to catch a ferry to Mazatlán in a few hours.

The ferry leaves from a place called Pichelingua, about 13 km from La Paz. At the port office, Brian and I book the group and the support jeep on board for the crossing, which will take seventeen hours. It costs well over a thousand dollars for everything and the price makes our sore heads even sorer. The ferry leaves at 5 p.m. Back in the hotel, we wake everyone else. Bikes are disassembled and stored in the back of the jeep for the ferry. A few taxis will take us all down to the port.

I use the spare time in La Paz to cash some travellers' cheques. La Paz is a modern town, full of American fast-food restaurants and other recognisable brands and logos.

For thirty minutes I wait in the bank, being referred back and forth between different officials who rubber stamp a number of documents. While I'm waiting, a deposit of money comes through the doors under heavily armed guard. A guard is handcuffed to a large briefcase and he's escorted into the bank by four guards armed with semi-automatic weapons. Two of the guards walk in front, their eyes glinting with fear. The other two are behind, walking backwards. Standard procedure, it seems, but you sense it's absolutely necessary. Armed authority makes me feel uneasy but, for everyone else in the bank, it's just another day.

As it turns out, the ferry is for cargo and not a passenger vessel as we thought. The crossing is mostly for truckers, for transporting goods back and forth to the mainland. No living quarters, no cabins, no restaurant, no television, bar or anything else to pass the time.

The Sea of Cortez is as still as a lake and the enormous orange sun sinks rapidly below the horizon and is replaced by a bright moon that shines a long yellow streak on the water.

Conversation and then a sing-song between us and some Mexican truckers starts up, amidst the trucks on the cargo deck.

'John Aldridge, Ireland v. Mexico USA 1994. You remember?' asks Sergio, a trucker from Juarez.

How can we forget? It's strange but most of them know the names of the Irish team that played that day.

EL Rosario

**Number of days on
the road: 87–88**

Number of kilometres completed: **7,833**

We arrive in Mazatlán at 9.30 a.m. With more ships at anchor on this side, the port is much bigger than Pichelingua. Like La Paz, the town is a short distance from the port, so we order a few taxis to get into town.

Mazatlán sprawls around an enormous bay on the Sea of Cortez. It seems even more westernised than La Paz, but when you walk a few blocks into the city, the true town reveals itself: decaying buildings, old women selling watermelons and groups of barefoot children playing football at the side of the streets. The touristy part of the town is empty. We've arrived in the rainy season and the place is dead.

Our two security escorts are replaced with two new men, Angel and Carlos. Mellie and Mickey are going home to Mexico City. Mellie is excited because he and his wife are expecting their first child any day. We thank them, present them each with a bottle of whiskey and wave them good-bye.

'*Bueno, hombres*; Good Irishmen. Good bye and God bless you all,' Mellie says.

Angel and Carlos are both in their mid-twenties. Angel spent a year at Ohio State University and speaks excellent English with a strong American accent. Carlos, like Mickey, doesn't speak English and is very shy. The two new guys drive off and find themselves a hotel. We spend the rest of the day at our hotel resting, watching movies and reassembling the bikes.

The next morning we're on the road early. The ferry crossing has taken us into the Tropic of Cancer and the landscape is different to that of Baja. On both sides of the road are lush, rolling green fields and thick vegetation. The countryside is softer: there's more agriculture, mostly livestock and poultry. Farmers herd cattle on horseback as we spin south. A continual string of people and settlements occupy both sides of the roads. We come to the town of El Rosario, our second one of this trip – one strange thing we've noticed is how a number of towns and villages have the same name. The town is heavily decorated with Mexican flags, ribbons and streamers. A stage and hundreds of white plastic chairs are set up in front of the town hall. Over the stage a banner reveals that 15 September is Mexican Independence Day (1808). There's a fiesta in town tonight.

'So we've stumbled on the Mexican St Patrick's Day?' Neil says.

'Wow, look at the women. Unbelievable!' says Rob.

The style is amazing. Young women are dressed in immaculate printed dresses with bright gold or silver belts.

On full display, they walk around the town's main square, showing off to the men who sit along the sides on benches. Occasionally, a man gets up and joins one of the girls; paired up, they continue to walk around the square together. It's an old courting ritual that must be older than the country's independence but none of us think it would be diplomatic to participate.

We finish our beers and walk back to the hotel. It would have been nice to stay out a while longer but, as usual, it's dawn patrol tomorrow.

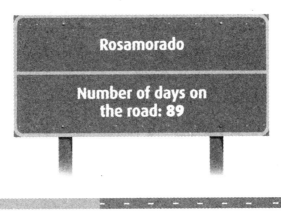

Rosamorado

Number of days on the road: 89

Number of kilometres completed: **7,961**

After 40 km of uninterrupted progress, Brian's front tyre blows out. Bang! Like a shotgun at point blank range. Progress grinds to a halt and when the wheel is inspected we see that the tyre is partly shredded. Alan replaces the tube and Brian cycles on for another couple of hundred metres before there's another loud pop and we have to dismount again. A new tyre is needed. The spare tyres are in the support jeep but it has already gone on ahead to the day's finishing point. With no other option, Brian hops into the FWG vehicle, and together with Angel and Carlos, drives to the next town, Acopolonet, to find a new tyre.

We follow them into town but there's no sign of a tyre that might fit the bike. Furthermore, there's no sign of Neil or the support jeep. Over lunch, we discuss what to do and eventually decide to split the group. John, Kev, Rob and I cycle on to Rosamorado and tell Neil that he'll have to drive back up the road in order to change Brian's tyre so Brian can get back on the road.

Rosamorado is recovering from its own Independence Day celebrations. Children's amusements remain by the town square. Green, white and red flags, banners and streamers line the walls of buildings and the white plastic chairs used to watch last night's entertainment are still outside.

Suddenly, it begins to rain. Streets turn into rivers and the water gushes around the debris and rubbish left over from last night. Loud claps of thunder shake the town and the atmosphere becomes dark and gloomy. The locals scurry indoors to bars and shops. We sit under a canopy outside an ice cream parlour, licking our cones, and watch the water cascade downwards, washing around the town's square.

Puerta Vallarta

Number of days on the road: 90–94

Number of kilometres completed: **8,241**

With the group back together, we continue down the road, headed for Puerta Vallarta, a large resort town on the Pacific. The road takes us into the mountains towards the Aztec city of Tepic. We climb upwards all day, causing a long line of traffic to build up behind. A steady line of traffic is coming the other way too, so it's dangerous for vehicles to overtake us.

Cillian isn't feeling well and every so often as he cycles behind me I hear him vomit. Continuing to climb slowly, we take an hour and a half before we reach the point where the road starts to descend. We pull into a lay-by to let the traffic backlog pass us and to take in the view of the Aztec country: dozens and dozens of rolling green mountains.

When the road flattens out, a police car passes us and pulls into the side of the road ahead of us. Three armed policemen get out of the car. The most senior of them, judging by his age, walks towards us.

He stares at us and purses his lip, as if something very serious has happened. He opens up into Spanish.

'I haven't a clue what this guy is saying,' says Alan.

'It doesn't sound great, whatever it is,' Brian says.

The FWG guys, who have pulled in behind us, jump out and begin to talk to the police. Translated through Angel, the policeman says that we have no licence or permit to cycle on the roads of Nayarit, the province of Mexico we're in. He says we can't cycle any further. Brian asks Angel whether it would be possible to sort things out right now but Angel says that it's not the time.

We're about 15 km from crossing into the next province, Jalisco, so we have to figure out a way to cross over without cycling. Once we're in the next state we'll become the responsibility of a different police force. When we cross over, we can cycle as much as we want for all they care, the policemen say.

They allow us to cycle another 2 km or so to the next small village in order to get us off the road. Driving right behind us, a loudspeaker from the car roars, *Mas Rapido*!

As the car comes even closer, we all speed up and start laughing.

In a small village, another one named San Francisco, we get off the bikes and the car pulls in behind us. Angel tells them that the support vehicle has gone on ahead of the group and that all of the bikes couldn't possibly fit into the FWG vehicle. In short, he tells them as diplomatically as possible that if we are not allowed to cycle on, we will require another large vehicle to transport our bikes over the provincial border, which is a problem that obviously hadn't occurred to the police. Without anything else being said, they get back into the car and speed off.

'Now what?' asks Cillian.

'Stay where you are guys; do what these men tell you,' Angel says.

'But they've just f***ed off; they haven't told us to do anything,' replies Cillian.

Minutes later the police car returns with a massive truck close behind it. Both vehicles pull in. The policemen jump out of their car, looking even less patient.

'Quickly. Out of here now,' says one, gesturing for us to get into the commandeered truck.

A vehicle used to transport tourists from Puerta Vallarta to surrounding off-road areas for hillwalking and white water rafting, the truck takes all the bikes and, in due course, deposits us all on the side of the road in Jalisco, about 10 km from Puerta Vallarta. It would have taken us twenty-five minutes to cycle the same distance.

Number of kilometres completed: **8,979**

Kieran O'Connor, the owner of FWG and a relation of Brian's, gets in touch and says that he'd like to meet up with us. He'll meet us at the seaside town of Ixtapa, 700 km south of Puerta Vallarta. We cycling through Jose Maria Oseles, Playa Puente and Tacanoma and, on 27 September, we arrive in Ziujuatanejo where we spend the night. We realise the following morning that Ixtapa is to the north of Ziujuatanejo. After breakfast, we cycle 15 km back up the road to the five-star Dorado Pacifico Hotel in Ixtapa.

Ixtapa is a government-planned tourist resort built in the early 1970s and constructed on what was once a coconut plantation and mangrove estuary. On the steps of the hotel we abandon our bikes and walk inside. No one has shaved in weeks and we're wearing filthy cycling gear. Hotel staff and guests cast strange looks in our direction.

'Jaysus, you look like you've cycled the distance alright. How are you all, lads?' says Kieran.

'We're not used to this craic,' Brian says.

'How many miles so far? Any problems? How are you all holding up physically?' Kieran asks, genuinely interested in what we have to say.

I'm able to show him my latest article in *The Irish Times*.

'Good man. I'd say you wouldn't mind a cocktail by the pool?' Kieran says.

After checking into our rooms and taking showers, the entire group has lunch on the terrace overlooking the hotel's private beach. Lily, who initially welcomed us to Mexico, has happily returned and we're also joined by Stefano, Kieran's head of operations in Mexico. At the end of lunch, Kieran makes a speech saying how delighted he is to be involved with such a great project and how inspiring he thinks the expedition is. Later, at dinner in a restaurant across the road from the hotel, I sit opposite Stefano, a man in his late fifties. His family moved to Mexico from Italy when he was a small child. He has long grey hair and tanned skin. Stefano speaks in quiet measured tones, which I imagine must be perfect for dealing with this country's gangs and authorities. We chat about his work and the problems FWG face.

'Gangs, police; it's all part of the job. This is Mexico. This is the way business works in Mexico,' he says.

When a cargo is being transported through areas known to be under gang control, a tariff is negotiated with the gang and freedom of passage provided. Stefano says that business with the gang leaders is generally conducted in a civilised manner, often in offices and over lunch, and that they normally always keep their ends of the bargain.

'No problem. Like negotiating with anyone else; maybe even more simple,' he says.

The cargoes FWG protect are high value goods such as computers and mobile phones. FWG are the best at what they do and the company has had an almost faultless delivery rate. All their cargoes carry GPS equipment, embedded during transit, so a cargo can be tracked down if it goes missing. Stefano says that only one cargo has gone missing in the history of the company and GPS tracked it down to a remote federal police warehouse.

'The police, the gangs; the same thing. They all want a piece of the cake,' Stefano says.

FWG have a policy to ensure that the trucks they escort are 'clean' and not in the business of transporting drugs. On one occasion, the company approached the police to ask if they could assist in checking a particular vehicle by providing a sniffer dog to inspect it. Strongly declining, the police stated that the truck was to be left alone and under no circumstances was it to be inspected. Notwithstanding this warning, the company carried out an inspection and discovered 60 kilos of marijuana stored under the seats in the cab of the truck.

Stefano speaks about these episodes as if it's daily business. The gangs are doing their job, the police are doing theirs and FWG is trying to operate between the two.

Conversation shifts to Colombia and to the threats we may be presented with. Whether or not FWG will accompany us through Colombia is still uncertain.

'My friend,' he says, 'I advise you, as a friend, not to cycle through Colombia.'

'But isn't Colombia safer now than it was? Lots of people are backpacking there now and I've heard it's quite safe to travel through the country,' I say.

Stefano leans back and laughs lightly. He then pauses and looks me straight in the eye.

'Your friends who tell you Colombia is safe sleep in the tourist hotels of Medellin, Cartagena and Bogota. Your route will take you through some of the most dangerous places in South America. There are checkpoints everywhere. You cannot tell who is official army and who is FARC (Revolutionary Armed Forces of Colombia, in Spanish, *Fuerzas Armadas Revolucionarias de Colombia*). Kidnap in this country is a huge problem. Trust me, my friend; Colombia for you ... no.'

Before now I hadn't thought about not going through Colombia. Skipping a country or taking any distance out of the journey is unthinkable. Stefano talks further about the security problems that Colombia would present. Certain parts of the country are controlled entirely by guerrillas. There are places where one simply cannot go. Stefano is fully aware of the details and full of other information too. He says that he knows for a fact that a 747 passenger jet flies from Bogota to Los Angeles International Airport every day, going offically unrecorded.

'But let's not talk so much about this. Enjoy the night. What about Ireland? I want to retire there with my daughter,' Stefano says.

He speaks of his desire for fresh air and horses for his daughter. Retiring in a place like Ireland is a dream because of the country's safety and peace. From my conversation with Stefano, I realise that even if we decide to cycle through Colombia, it won't be with the protection of FWG. The group moves from the restaurant to a bar next door. After a drink or two, I decide to walk back to the hotel. It's not often we sleep in five-star beds.

Puerto Escondido

Number of days on the road: 103–106

Number of kilometres completed: **9,369**

Kieran, Stefano and Lily leave the hotel on the 29th and fly back to Mexico City. We check out of the hotel the next morning and return to Zihuatanejo. When we get back to the cheap motel, the one where the two FWG escorts have been staying for the past few days, the five-star treatment seems like a dream. A large fishing town, Zihuatanajo, overlooks a harbour that's almost completely enclosed and sheltered from the South Pacific. Dozens of restaurants are dotted along the harbour front where fishermen sell their catch directly from their boats.

The following morning we continue down the coast, headed for Puerto Escondido, a place we've heard a lot about. It's a well-known surfers' hang-out and a place that attracts large numbers of backpackers. After Tecpan we are now in the province of Guerrero, a notoriously dangerous part of Mexico, according to Angel. Angel says that as you travel south, the country tends to become even more lawless.

We arrive in Puerto Escondido on 2 October and check into Hostel Mayflower, which overlooks the bay. The hostel is full of backpackers from all over the world: Australians, Dutch, Germans, English and Americans. Now it's dominated by Irish. We'll stay here for six days. This was always the plan. We're ahead of schedule. Alan's girlfriend, Timi, arrives from Ireland and plans to bike with us to Panama City.

I ring home on the morning of 3 October.

'Things are going really well. We're on schedule. How are things at home?' I ask.

'Fine, fine,' my dad says. 'But the country is in trouble.'

'Trouble? Why?'

'The economy was nearly wiped out overnight; the government guaranteed all the banks' deposits; it's a bloodbath here, the banks are going under.'

I think back over the past two weeks. No one seems to have been in contact with any family or friends until yesterday or today. We hadn't heard anything about banks.

'What are you guys up to at the moment?' Dad asks.

'We're in a surf town. No one here seems to have heard about what's going on at home. I'm thinking of going deep-sea fishing tomorrow. We're back on the bikes soon. We're just taking a few days off.'

Dad wishes us luck and says everyone is thinking of us. It's hard to imagine, sitting here in the peaceful sunshine, that the world is not all like this.

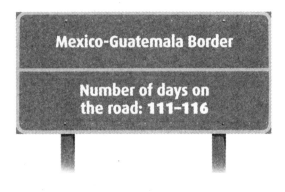

Mexico–Guatemala Border

Number of days on the road: 111–116

Number of kilometres completed: **10,264**

My birthday is on 8 October. I'm twenty-three years old. The lads ask me if I'd like to take another day off to celebrate but I want to get going again. I don't want my birthday to hold up our progress.

Angel and Carlos swap with yet two more FWG personnel, Antonio and Jesus. Antonio is definitely the more senior of the two. He's about thirty years old, wears long baggy shorts and a rag tied to his head. A toothpick hangs constantly from his lip. Jesus is the quiet member of the duo. Younger than Antonio, he makes no real attempt to talk to us and spends most of his time in the jeep.

'We follow you. Let's go!' says Antonio.

We leave Escondido with two extra cyclists whom we met during our time there. Peter is from Nova Scotia, he'll be with us until Panama, and Sebastian, whom John met in a bar last night, is from Lyon in France. They cycle our two spare bikes that we keep in the back of the trailer. Combined with the arrival of Timi, we are now ten cyclists in total.

Eighty kilometres from Escondido we check into a run-down old farm building, advertised as a hotel and take three rooms. Nights have been spent in junkyards, back gardens, restaurant floors and garages, yet this place is the worst yet. Buckets and spades and other farmyard clutter are in the bathrooms and the windows in the bedrooms are shattered. The walls are damp and the paint is peeling. Chickens roam around the corridors and their faeces, along with dirt and straw, is scattered on the floor. The best thing to do is get to sleep as quickly as possible and leave before sunrise.

The next morning we move out early. Sebastian has had enough already, it seems, and Neil drives him back to Escondido. A tough first day cycling out of Escondido topped off with a night at the hotel from hell undoubtedly brought about his change of heart but it's better that he leaves now rather than in a few days. We shake hands, wish him all the best and are on our way again. Sebastian is the first casualty of the Pan American Cycle Test, the first person to give up and he did it so easily.

We press on down the coast to the poor town of Santiago Astata and check into Hotel Paris. Scrambled eggs and tortillas are cooked by the landlady. We are now in the province of Oaxaca. During dinner, Antonio, our new FWG escort, informs me that this province, not far from the Guatemala border, is the poorest and most dangerous of all. I tell him that it seems that every province we enter is more dangerous than the last one.

Oaxaca is the gateway to Mexico from the subcontinent

of Central America. The province is part of a well-established route for the trafficking of cocaine which starts from Colombia and Bolivia and then passes through the Central American countries and into the United States. Antonio says that though, traditionally, this is how things work, cocaine is now beginning to be manufactured within Mexico and particularly in this province. His English is extremely limited but he tries very strongly to convey the danger to us.

'*Peligrosa*?' I ask. 'Is it dangerous?'

'*Si, peligrosa. Mucho peligrosa.*'

It rains heavily as we cycle towards the Guatemalan border; the rain is different from the rain we are familiar with at home. Thick sheets of water fall hard from the sky, saturating everything instantly. Surrounding fields take the form of lakes in which drenched children fish with hand-made rods and nets and the deluge turns the road into a slippery river. Young fishermen turn around and stop everything to wave to us. Bright white smiles beam across the fields.

Towns flash by: Salina Cruz, La Vendoza and on the evening of 10 October we find ourselves in the town of Juchitan where we pay $20 for the floor of a restaurant for the night. Paul, Andrew and Jenny leave the group and catch a bus to the Caribbean coastline. They've been with us for a good long stretch and have been great fun to have around. The support team is reduced. The next days bring us through the towns of Arriaga, Tapachula and eventually to the border town of Hidalgo; it's the end of Oaxaca and, indeed, of Mexico.

GUATEMALA

13–16 October 2008

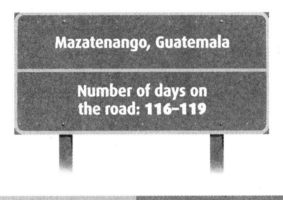

Mazatenango, Guatemala

Number of days on
the road: 116–119

Number of kilometres completed: **10,392**

For seven weeks we have travelled freely through Mexico. We've never really been delayed crossing a border. As we approach the border between Mexico and Guatemala, I sense that our free run is coming to an end.

In Tapichula, the FWG guys click into a more serious mode. They tell us to stay together and warn us to be even more mindful of security on the Guatemalan side.

A wide dirty river – Rio Naranjo – divides Mexico and Guatemala. The banks of the river are thick with people washing clothes and fishing in the filthy water. Our passports are stamped and we pass out of Mexico and cycle over the bridge to Guatemala. Antonio jogs behind us and we gather in front of the Guatemalan customs office.

153

'Friends; this is my job. Please leave things to me,' he says.

Apparently, it's not going to be a case of simply having the passports stamped. Ten minutes later, the support jeep pulls into a nearby car park. Neil and Antonio approach Guatemalan customs with the necessary documents needed, including all our passports. Children with torn clothes, wearing no shoes, beg for money. A stench of rubbish fills the air. Locals offer their border 'expertise' in exchange for a fee.

'Things aren't moving that quickly. The Guatemalans

Alan Gray *(right)* leads the way as we cycle out of Mexico and into Guatemala: there are rainier and more dangerous times ahead.

are looking for a document for the jeep that I've never even heard about. The jeep won't be allowed to pass through without it,' says Neil.

Antonio is angry.

'*Buda* Guatemala!' he says repeatedly, pacing alone, just ahead of us.

Officials are laying the foundations for a bribe, inventing procedures until we ask them if anything can be done to speed things up. As gringos with expensive bikes and a $15,000 jeep, we are in a very poor bargaining position. Since we are between two countries, they know we'll have to cough up in order to continue. The question is not whether we'll pay or not; it's when and how much.

'Patience, friends. This is normal here,' says Antonio.

He throws his eyes to heaven and curses the Guatemalans yet again. He makes several further attempts, broken by long pauses, until a price (about $100) to enable us to cross over is settled upon and the document, so vital to our trip only an hour and a half ago, is forgotten about. By the time we cycle into Guatemala it's dark. Locals gather outside shops and taco bars, chatting and smoking. We take the first hotel we find and Antonio and the hotel's owner advise us not to spend too much time outside on the streets. In a nearby restaurant, we have a quick bite to eat before heading back to our rooms.

Our first impressions of Guatemala aren't good as we set out the next morning: it's much poorer than Mexico, the villages and towns are run down without even the occasional signs of affluence that we saw over the past six weeks. Halfway through the day, sitting outside a small roadside restaurant after lunch, we chat with an American guy called Juan. Juan emigrated to the US from Guatemala as a young child. Now, he works for the US army in Iraq as a driver of a fuel truck in supply convoys. He is wearing an expensive pair of sunglasses, designer clothes and speaks with a Boston accent. Within five minutes of describing his job, he says he reckons the best thing you can do at the moment is to buy Iraqi currency to take advantage of the potential improvement when the Iraqi economy stabilises (a practice prohibited by the US armed forces). Americans never take long to tell you everything about themselves.

'Anyone working out there who has a clue is buying it. Guys are coming home to the States with suitcases and gym bags full of it,' he says.

We chat about Guatemala, its poverty and its other problems. Juan is saddened at how the country has deteriorated in the past ten years. It wasn't this bad when he was a child, he claims, saying that an increase in drug-related crime has torn the country apart. Successive governments have done nothing to improve the situation and there's corruption at every level. It's the same story all over Central America, Juan says.

He tells us that the road we're going to take, the Pacific Coast Highway, runs to the end of the country but doesn't show off the best of Guatemala. Our route passes through some of the country's poorest regions and towns.

'Take a couple of days off and travel up into the mountains. See the lakes and volcanoes. Go water skiing or rent a kayak for a few hours. Staying on the Pacific coast road won't show you the best of Guatemala,' he says.

We say goodbye to Juan and get back on the road. At

the end of the day we arrive in Mazatenango and it's even worse than the border. Armed security men are stationed outside every business along the main street. Two men with semi-automatic weapons keep guard outside a bakery.

Trucks carrying consignments of Coca-Cola pass by. Armed guards lie on the cargoes of soft drink, protecting them against a hijack. Nothing is safe. Everyone is constantly on guard. We check into a hotel and lock the bikes away in an outhouse for the night. No one has advised us not to go into town but none of us seems keen to do so anyway. With all the danger, the rain and the humidity, things haven't been so enjoyable recently. Our spirits are low.

'Let's get out of here for a couple of days and head up into the mountains and have a night out to relax,' says Alan.

I'm worried what effect this will have on our progress but what's the point in passing through Guatemala if we're locked up in hotel rooms every night? We decide we'll leave the bikes where they are, head into the mountains and start cycling again from here in two days. The following day, we pile into the two jeeps and head inland into the mountains. Panajachel is on Lake Atitlan, a place Juan had mentioned. Everybody's mood lifts. For two and a half hours the road winds uphill. Clapped-out bangers overtake us on dangerous bends. Locals leave no space between themselves and other vehicles. It's bumper to bumper and, often, as a car attempts to overtake, it stays on the other lane for far too long, creating white knuckle situations. The drop down from the road is sheer. Dotted on either side are crosses indicating fatalities.

'I'm genuinely fearing for my life,' says Cillian.

As we get higher, the towering volcanoes pop up along

the horizon and the lakes, like mirrors, nestle beneath them, just as Juan said. Locals are selling brightly coloured rugs, shawls and other souvenirs. These people have dark faces, are of much smaller stature and seem not to be of European extraction, like the people on the coast. Two women, dressed in bright, multicoloured shawls and wearing hats, carry bundles of sticks on their backs. Behind them, a donkey pulls a man sitting on a small cart.

We check into basic hotel accommodation at Panajachel, very near the shore of Lake Atitlan. With plenty of westerners around, it looks like it's one of Guatemala's top tourist spots. After dinner, we have a beer in a bar on the main strip where we are pestered relentlessly by the locals to buy souvenirs and drugs. We decide to go back to the hotel for some peace and quiet.

EL SALVADOR

17–21 October 2008

Zacatecoluca, El Salvador

Number of days on
the road: 120–124

Number of kilometres completed: **10,552**

It's back to business. We leave Mazetenango and head for
Escuintla. I get two punctures, very frustrating. The tube has
already been patched six times and is now useless. Only a
couple of tubes are left; the particular type we need hasn't
been available in any of the bike shops we've come across in
Mexico or Guatemala. Eric, who left the group in San
Francisco, has sent more to San José, Costa Rica, where Neil
will pick them up in the jeep. Until then, we have to make
do with what we have.

In a small roadside restaurant, the bathroom sink is full
of small crabs, and hens scratch around on the floor
between our feet. The town of Escuintla reveals a poverty
we haven't yet seen on the road. On the main street, which
is dense with people, beggars in their dozens lie out on the

road, some with amputated legs or arms, others suffering from horrific skin diseases. Armed security is everywhere: outside restaurants, internet cafés and butcher's shops. Buildings are dilapidated; plaster work peels off the sides of walls, and the roads are not paved. Rainwater, thick with refuse and other waste, cascades through the town. We check into a hotel called Hotel Costa Sur, positioned behind enormous steel gates and venture out for something to eat. Myself, Alan, Brian and John sit in a restaurant eating chicken and chips and watch the rain pour down.

The next day we make our way towards the El Salvador border, happy to be moving on. If ever I return to Guatemala, it won't be to any of the places along this stretch of road. What was I expecting? I thought it would be a gradual continuation of Mexico, but I've been shocked by the acute poverty, the destitution of large portions of the population and the constant sense of danger in the towns.

The border is yet another example of Guatemala's impoverishment. It is littered with children begging for money and people trying to rip off tourists that pass through, guaranteeing that, for a small fee, they can ensure a quick passage into El Salvador. Other locals say they can get the best exchange rate. You're never left alone. If you're a westerner – a gringo – you've got a dollar bill sign permanently on your head.

We pass into El Salvador without hassle; it just takes a lot of time. Antonio's and Jesus' days with the group are over. Antonio has been a huge help at the borders.

'Stay safe, *amigos*. Tell me when you are finished,' says Antonio.

Antonio and Jesus are replaced by two new security guys from San Salvador, the capital city of El Salvador; Marcello and José. Only twenty-two years old, Marcello is an ex-soldier. Jose, in his late thirties, is a huge fat man who must weigh at least 20 stone. When we first meet him, he's out of breath and constantly wiping sweat from his brow. The changeover is brief and progress continues. At the border to El Salvador, we are told that there's a free-movement-of-people-agreement among El Salvador, Honduras, Nicaragua and Costa Rica; the 'Central American Four', as they're called. Essentially, the visa you get for El Salvador allows you to move around these four countries as much as you want for ninety days. With luck, this will mean that we won't get held up much at the borders over the next couple of weeks.

Unlike in Guatemala, the Pacific coast road in El Salvador hugs the coastline. The road in Guatemala was always a few kilometres inland but here the ocean views are spectacular. Like Highway 101 in California, the road surfaces are immaculate.

In 1992, El Salvador emerged from a twelve-year civil war in which over 75,000 people died. The US backed the right-wing government, which fought against a collaboration of left-wing extremists and guerrillas. Peace resulted in considerable inward investment and access to international finance markets to facilitate the country's redevelopment. Guatemala hasn't experienced such a recent catastrophe on that scale. The slick tarmac roads we now find ourselves cycling on are the result of the civil strife. Countries that have destroyed themselves through conflict are often the quickest to turn things around and political choices determine your future.

On the morning of the 20th, Alan comes into the large bedroom where we're sleeping and tries to get everyone up. It's clear Cillian is not well. Though some of us are ready to go we decide to cancel cycling for the day and allow Cillian some time to feel better and build back up some energy.

Fifty kilometres inside El Salvador, we stop at a restaurant on a cliff where we order calamari and steak. No one is around hassling us for money or selling anything. After a night in the town of Zacatecoluca, we continue along the flat, fast roads, volcanoes to the east, lakes and wide flats between us and the Pacific. We set into a forty-minute climb. At the top, we dismount and look back upon the ocean, the flat ground and the volcanoes, which form one panoramic vista.

After lunch, we cycle on to the Honduran border. Brian's not feeling well and most of the group have diarrhoea; maybe the calamari and steak weren't so great after all. We'll cross tomorrow morning. Central America is passing by in a flash. It shows how small these countries are but this thought reminds me of the size of the US, Canada and Mexico.

We pose for another group shot at the border of El Salvador, *(l–r):* Ben, Alan Gray, Cillian O'Shea, John Garry, Rob Greene, Brian McDermott, Peter Haeghaert and Kevin Hillier.

NICARAGUA

22–23 October 2008

León, Nicaragua

Number of days on the road: 125–126

Number of kilometres completed: **11,128**

We aim to leave El Salvador, pass through Honduras and enter Nicaragua all in about ten hours.

To pass into Honduras we're charged $7 each and $107 for the support jeep. What happened to the free movement agreement throughout the Central American Four?

Most of the group are suffering from fatigue, sickness and diarrhoea but, at the moment, I'm in good shape. I can't remember the last time everyone felt 100 per cent at the same time.

El Salvador has a long Pacific coastline. It borders Honduras, which has a very small Pacific coastline of just 130 km, even though Honduras is a far bigger country. The majority of the territory of Honduras lies to the north of El Salvador. Honduras has a very long Caribbean coastline whereas El Salvador does not have any contact with the Caribbean.

The sky darkens and black clouds begin to rumble. An electrical storm engulfs us and it rains torrentially. Huge streaks of forked lightning streak across the sky. Dark hills, kilometres in the distance, illuminate for fractions of seconds at a time. Water from the road sprays into our faces as we peddle south towards Nicaragua.

Soaked to the bone, we arrive at the border. Neil is there already, arranging for the jeep to cross. He met two guys from California who have driven down from LA. Neil's been talking to them about Colombia and the best way to get the jeep over there. The Americans are giving Colombia a miss; they're heading straight for Ecuador instead but say that whether we pass though Colombia or not, the support jeep will have to be shipped from Panama to a point in South America anyway. You cannot drive from Panama to Colombia; no roads exist between the two countries. The Panamanian province of Darian, an area of thick jungle dividing Central and South America, is one of the most impenetrable and dangerous parts of the world, the Americans told Neil.

There has always been a question mark hanging over cycling through Colombia. Brian is in contact with a man called Luiz in the FWG office in Mexico City and from what I can gather, he's confirming that we just can't cycle through. FWG aren't prepared to escort us if we enter Colombia and it seems that no other private security companies are interested in taking the risk either. If we cycle through Colombia, we'll be on our own.

On 23 October, we push on another 116 km towards the

Nicaraguan town of León. Some stress from sickness is lingering in the group. Taking an easy morning, we set off when everyone is comfortable to go. The huge amount of rain over the past days has left the countryside flooded. Kids splash around on both sides of the road and women make the most of the situation by washing clothes in the flood water. Everyone we pass smiles and waves and you can hear the kids shouting, '*Hola, Gringo!*'

The Bigfoot Hostel in León is full of European backpackers. Arriving at these places gives us a chance to slide into the backpacker lifestyle for a night or two. This hostel has a television and a DVD player. Rob, Kev and I watch *Hostel* followed by *Wolf Creek*, a combination that leaves the three of us terrified as we go to bed.

Day 127 Peter Haeghaert and Ben cycle into León in Nicaragua.

COSTA RICA

24 October – 1 November 2008

Jaco Beach, Costa Rica

Number of days on
the road: 127–135

Number of kilometres completed: **11,368**

We're coming to the end of the North American continent, a fact that really hits me only today. What am I thinking about the prospect of cycling the length of another continent? I am excited about South America. I feel fit and strong and I am looking forward to the next months. Our time in Central America has been difficult. Sickness and problems with the bikes meant the mood in the camp hasn't always been at its highest. The road has taken us through dangerous areas and the hassle at the borders hasn't helped. Since we've been cycling in the middle of the rainy season, we've been arriving at the end of most days like drowned rats. We have been battling hard.

The road from León, tracking Lake Nicaragua, takes us

through Managua, the capital, where the Nicaraguan presidential election campaign is in full swing. Supporters of David Ortega are campaigning loudly; his election posters are on almost every telegraph pole. Ortega's been a part of Nicaraguan politics for decades and has formed alliances with Iran and the FARC of Colombia. A left-wing radical, he's not a favourite of the Americans.

A climb out of Managua is followed by a 15 km drop into the colonial town of Granada. There's a noticeable contrast between the capital city and Granada; Managua is very much a poor, dangerous Central American city but Granada appears to be relatively wealthy, with beautiful colonial buildings and plenty of tourists. We book into a hostel called La Libertad and, because we're not cycling tomorrow, have a few beers.

Back home, Mum, Dad and my sister Jessica are preparing an auction for next weekend to raise money for our bike charity. The charity deals with a number of small projects in sub-Saharan Africa and always works in partnership with local enterprises. We've focused on Kenya because Kev grew up there. We've singled out a few projects we wish to help: the building of a rock damn in Lodwar, supporting the Girl Child Network (which helps young girls stay in school) and the building of an orphanage in the northern town of Kisumu.

Brian, Kev and I make a short DVD discussing our progress on the road and talking about the charity. I'll email it home and hope it'll make things a bit more real to the people who show up at the weekend auction. Although we're doing this cycle for ourselves, first and foremost, the charity is becoming increasingly more important. The cycling will come to an end but I reckon the funds raised will become the trip's legacy. Hitting our target of €200,000 might be a lot harder than the cycle itself, given the way things are at home.

On 26 October we leave Granada and make our way towards Costa Rica, 105 km away. In a restaurant at the border, everyone is glued to a baseball game, Tampa Bay v Philadelphia. We pay for our food in US dollars: Costa Rica is a major tourist destination for Americans. McDonald's, Burger King, Starbucks and Quiznos are advertised constantly. Kilometre signs indicate distances from Quiznos and McDonald's. Only 15 km to McDonald's! Hot Starbucks coffee in 20 km!

In contrast to this splurge of commercialism is the fantastic wildlife that we see in Costa Rica. Brightly coloured parrots fly high throughout the dense canopy of trees and an anteater sits just off the road, lifting its head to reveal its long snout.

From La Cruz, we cycle towards the town of Liberia. The coastline is gentler and, it seems, as we approach the end of North America, that the continent's landscape is becoming less difficult to pass through. We check into Hostel Liberia where there is only one other guest, a middle-aged South African called John. The hostel has a large television room, so Alan, Kev and I find ourselves with John watching Fox News. The US Presidential election is winding up: Obama is ahead in almost every single poll and the last time I checked on Paddy Power he was 1/10 to win. Fox is giving almost no attention to Obama's campaign and when they do focus on it the commentary is extremely negative.

Tired and dirty, we smile for the obligatory group shot at the border of Costa Rica, *(l–r):* Ben, Alan Gray, John Garry, Kevin Hillier, Cillian O'Shea, Peter Haeghaert, Rob Greene and Brian McDermott.

John is incensed at this and screams at the television. 'F***ing Fox bastards! Why don't you say it like it really is?'

The footage cuts to interviews with people throughout the mid-west and the southern states of America who say they're concerned that Obama, if elected, will turn the United States into a socialist state: universal health care is a bad thing and Obama isn't tough enough on terrorism. All the while, John roars abuse at the television and explains to us the untruths of Fox News.

Over the next days, the road takes us through Cañas and Esperanza and on 29 October, directed by distance signs sponsored by Subway, we arrive in the seaside town of Jaco Beach. The town is one long strip of restaurants, bars and retail units running parallel to the beach. American real estate agents, Century 21, display local properties for sale.

PANAMA

2–21 November 2008

Panama City

Number of days on
the road: **136–155**

Number of kilometres completed: **12,080**

We leave Jaco Beach and pass through Playa Dominical, Uvita and Paso Canoas and, on 4 November, we reach the Costa Rican border with Panama. The clocks now go forward as we cross the frontier, all the time getting closer to Greenwich Mean Time. The roads in Panama are better than in Costa Rica with pale concrete surfaces rather than tarmac. About 45 km inside the country, we stop for an early lunch in the town of David.

It's been pouring rain all day and we're soaked. Local men wearing Panama hats are out working in the fields. The hats have black and white stripes, not like the plain cream ones we're used to seeing in Ireland and England. Apparently, the Panama hat has its origins in Ecuador, where it was first worn. President Theodore Roosevelt wore the hat on a much publicised visit to Panama to inspect the construction of the canal and, thereafter, the hat adopted Panama rather than Ecuador as its name.

We stop for the night in the town of Tolé. At a local restaurant, the US election results, state by state, are showing on two televisions: it's looking good for Obama. We go back to where we are staying with the result all but a certainty. Obama is the next President of the US. John can't believe it; he owes me $100!

From Tolé, it's 190 km to Panama City. Keen to finish it out in one day, we set out on 6 November to finish up North America. It will be FWG's last day with us too. We've been told about a climb called Death Valley, about 100 km to the north of Panama City. Some locals have tried to persuade us to change routes and avoid it. We can't establish whether the road is dangerous from a security point of view or just very steep and difficult to climb. Either way, it can't be avoided easily and eventually we take it – a straight-forward 3 km climb. Some roads are talked about more than others and rumours about dangerous climbs are usually exaggerated. Safety on the road is mostly about concentration. Falls happen when you take your mind off things for too long.

Increased traffic and billboards indicate we haven't far to go to Panama City. Skyscrapers in the distance begin to glow in the dusk and the bridge over the Panama Canal sticks out prominently. Climbing to the apex of the bridge, we cross over the canal and then freewheel into the city. At about 8 p.m., we reach Luna's Castle Hostel and dismount the bikes for the last time in North America.

Straight away, Brian tries to find out whether or not anyone is prepared to provide a security escort for us in Colombia. At the moment, the plan to cycle through Colombia is still on.

Brian has a three-way phone conversation with Luiz and Kieran, who's back home in Ireland. FWG can't get us permits to travel through Colombia. The Colombian army and police force want nothing to do with us. Kieran says we're too high risk; we'd be sitting ducks for a kidnapping. Both Luiz and Kieran plead with Brian to consider shipping straight to Ecuador, giving Colombia a miss. Luiz says a dozen bodies were discovered on the Venezuelan border a number of days ago and tensions are particularly high at the moment. Colombian authorities are under pressure to register a certain amount of arrests every year – positive quotas – and often, it is alleged, they will arrest innocent people, mostly from inner-city slums, bring them to remote parts of the country, dress them in guerrilla uniforms and then execute and bury them. The process will appear as a police victory in the newspapers in the following days.

Luiz makes contact with the Colombian Cycling Federation to see if they would provide an escort but they also say no; it's too late in the day.

On the morning of 7 November Alan, Kev, Brian and I meet over lunch to decide finally on Colombia. Initially, we all think we should push on anyway; Colombia is part of the plan and none of us want to make a shortcut. Complete the trip as it was planned; that's what we want. Part of our publicity before we left home was that our trip would be different because, unlike similar trips, we would be passing through Colombia. All others gave it a miss.

Ben (left) and Alan Gray pose in torrential rain at the Panama Welcome Sign.

But there's more at stake than ourselves; we're responsible for the welfare of the group, the integrity of our sponsors and the charity, to get to the end of the road and to arrive home safely in March.

Our families soon find out what's going on and it's not long before our parents, who've all been speaking to each other, make contact, urging us not to go. They're all saying the same thing: if you finish the trip, no one will know if you cycled through Colombia or not.

'It's now or never, lads. Those that want to go should go and those that don't should fly straight to Ecuador and wait there. People at home are saying no one will remember skipping Colombia; I'll remember skipping Colombia,' says Kev.

'But how can we go when all the advice we're getting is telling us not to? How little respect does that show everyone?' I say.

'The group is staying together,' says Alan, ending the possibility of a split.

No one wants to make the final call. No one wants to admit defeat. After an hour of further discussion, we decide to skip Colombia, thereby cutting around 2,500 km off our journey's total distance. It hurts badly. We'll ship the jeep and bikes straight to Ecuador.

Cycling through Colombia would have taken more than two weeks. Making the decision to cut it out means we have spare time on our hands. After telling the lads that we're giving Colombia a miss, attention turns to how we're going to ship the jeep and the bikes to Guayaquil, Ecuador.

The port offices in Panama are chaotic. After a couple of days and, having made no progress, we realise we need a translator. Our FWG escorts have driven back to El Salvador. We stay in a hostel called Luna's Castle, run by a group of young Americans. There we meet Chris from Belfast. A tall, thin, unshaven guy with long hair, he's in his late twenties. He's broke and has been hanging around,

Day 170 We cycle single file in Peru, *(l–r):* Rob Greene, John Garry, Ben, Cillian O'Shea and Alan Gray.

Day 176 A digger makes easy work of clearing sand off the road in northern Peru.

Day 206 Ben takes a shaded nap just north of Antofagasta.

Day 211 We set up camp in the Atacama Desert in Chile.

Day 212 Cycling along an unpaved road in the Atacama Desert.

Day 220 We cycle past rows of vines as we climb towards the
Chile–Argentina border.

Day 221 Ben concentrates on the road ahead as the group reaches the Chile–Argentina border.

Day 221 We made it! The hairpins on the approach to the Chile–Argentina border are stacked like stairs, one on top of the other.

Day 242 We take a pit-stop in Patagonia, *(l–r):* John Garry, Brian McDermott, Ben Leonard Kane, Mark Gray, Kevin Hillier, Neil McDermott, Paul Drysdale, Alan Gray and Ben.

Day 244 The sleeping arrangements still aren't luxurious. Here we 'make camp' near Puerto Madryn in Patagonia.

Day 243 In Patagonia, we must compete for space with huge trucks
(and unforgiving drivers).

Day 243 The road in Patagonia stretches to the horizon, *(l–r):* Alan Gray, Ben Leonard Kane, Brian McDermott, John Garry and Paul Drysdale.

Day 260 At the finish line in Ushuaia, Argentina, *(back row, l–r):* Rob Green, Ben, and John Garry; *(front row, l–r):* Alan Gray, Cillian O'Shea, Kevin Hillier and Brian McDermott.

unable to move on from Panama for weeks. Hostel accommodation comes with a complimentary breakfast of pancakes and this is the only food Chris has been living on.

'I hear you boys are in need of a Spanish speaker,' he says.

'Yeah, we haven't a clue what's going on down in the port; we're getting nowhere,' Alan says.

'I'm fluent. I'll help you with the negotiation if you like.'

We agree to buy Chris' lunch every day and Brian and Neil say they'll lend him money for an airfare to Colombia in exchange for his help.

In order to arrange for everything to be shipped to Ecuador, we must book a container on a ship. Port officials require documents to be stamped by a number of different divisions of the police. The pace of work and the processing of information in Panamanian bureaucracy is staggeringly slow. Without Chris, it would be impossible.

Slowing progress even further is the incredible number of public holidays in the Panamanian calendar. More often than not, the offices are closed, so we return to the hostel and wait around until the next day. There's nothing we can do; without shipping the support jeep, we can't continue. Much time is spent in the hostel chatting to other guests, reading and just hanging around.

Luna's Castle is a busy hostel and full of different characters and oddballs. Some have been here for months. Others, like Chris, are stuck here. Sprinkled in between are those who stay for a couple of nights and move on quickly; English gap students, UCD arts students. An American woman called Charlotte, who's about thirty, and her boyfriend, Jake, have been staying here for the past few weeks. Charlotte is a hairdresser and works out of her room in the hostel. I'm happy to let her give my hair a trim.

'So where in the States are you from?' I ask, as I sit down and she places a towel around my neck.

'Oh, y'know, all over.'

'Cool, and when are you going home?' I ask, trying to make conversation as she sprays and combs my hair.

'I don't think I'll ever be going home.'

I sense there's a serious reason for this and so stay quiet.

'I'm not welcome back in the United States,' Charlotte says, laughing. 'If I go back, I'll be living in jail.'

'Oh right! What happened?'

'You're Irish, right? Well, I was caught with a kilo of cocaine in Florida on St Patrick's Day this year. My boyfriend and I dyed the coke green. People loved it – thought it was great fun. We jumped bail. Now we're here.'

'What are you going to do?'

'Well, we're not going to go to jail!' Charlotte says.

It's ten days since we made the decision not to cycle through Colombia and little progress has been made with the shipping arrangements. Eventually, on Chris' advice, we employ a 'port liaison', a local man you pay to skip queues and pay off the port authorities. From then on, things start running quickly: a container is booked and a date is set for shipping everything to Ecuador. A full container is more than enough room for all our equipment, so we wait for a number of days to see if anyone might appear who would be interested in sharing. When no one is forthcoming, we close and seal the container ourselves and make for the airport to fly out of Panama and into South America, at last.

COLOMBIA

22 November–3 December 2008

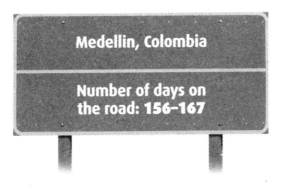

Medellin, Colombia

Number of days on the road: 156–167

Number of kilometres completed: **12,080**

Although we haven't been able to cycle through Colombia, that doesn't mean we can't check it out. With the time it's going to take to ship the jeep and bikes to Ecuador, we have some time to ourselves. We fly into Medellin.

Medellin is situated amidst mountains, which gives it the appearance of a stadium or amphitheatre. Following the hostelling trail, we stay in The Wild Rover, an Irish-owned and run hostel. It's full of other backpackers. There's a pool and a busy bar.

Medellin was home of the infamous, now deceased, drug dealer Pablo Escobar, once listed by Forbes as the seventh wealthiest man in the world. The story goes that he used to store vast quantities of cash in warehouses, where

Day 156 We take another group shot and this time we're at Panama Airport about to board our flight to Colombia, *(l–r):* Cillian O'Shea, Rob Greene, Brian McDermott, Neil McDermott, Alan Gray, Ben and John Garry.

tens of thousands of dollars were annually destroyed by rodents. The Medellin Cartel, which Escobar ran, killed hundreds of people and was the first major exporter of cocaine from Colombia to the US.

Escobar's reputation is ambiguous here because, although he was such a notorious criminal, he invested heavily in local housing and public infrastructure. We take a trip to his grave, a small journey outside the city, where he is buried in the Escobar family plot. Quite a normal plot, it is frequently visited by tourists intrigued by Escobar's life.

After one night in Medellin, everyone except for Cillian and myself, who hang around for another night, takes a bus to Quito, the capital of Ecuador.

On 25 November, Cillian and I take a bus for Ipiales, a town just shy of the border with Ecuador. From here, the plan is to catch another bus to Quito. In all, it's approximately a twenty-two hour journey. Climbing up and around mountain roads, the bus drops to a snail's pace in parts, stopping at road blocks as it gets farther south. Drifting in and out of sleep from the sleeping tablet I've taken, I hear only the hum of the bus' engine. We stop and I wake, in a sleepy daze, to find a Colombian soldier with a machine gun standing directly over me, rooting through my back pack.

'Passport,' he says.

I rummage through my bag but see he already has my passport in his hands and is looking through it for my Colombian entry stamp. After a few seconds and a long glare, he hands it back.

'*Gracias.*'

In the town of Pasto, the bus stops and the driver's voice on the PA system tells us to get off and wait in the bus station. He says there has been some 'unrest' in the town but that the problem shouldn't be too serious and we'll soon get going again.

We collect our bags from the luggage stowage area and go directly to the bus station's departure lounge. There's a lot of noise coming from nearby: protesting voices and loud bangs. Suddenly, police with large shields and batons surround the bus station. Directly in front of where we are, we can see people on the streets with posters and placards, chanting rhythmically.

An English couple in their mid-thirties, Mark and Tara, are stuck too. Both are teachers from London. An organised pair of travellers, they're kitted out with expensive rucksacks and hiking boots. Tara seems to be worried but Mark gives the appearance of being calm.

'Well, this wasn't part of the plan, was it?' he says with cool understatement.

'What the hell is all this about?' I ask.

'Apparently, a government investment scheme went belly-up as a result of the recent global economic collapse,' says Mark. 'Seems like people may have lost a few pesos. A bank on Wall Street goes bust and a town in Colombia explodes.'

A couple of hundred people are positioned about a hundred metres from the bus station. Noise of the protest becomes louder and suddenly the people around us scatter. Plumes of white smoke fill the building and we're all coughing and spluttering. My eyes sting. With my arm to my face, covering my mouth and nose, I run to the exit for fresh air but the police quickly usher me back inside. There's a riot going on here but why they're focusing on the bus station is anyone's guess.

The police tell us that no buses will now leave Pasto until 7 a.m. tomorrow morning, twelve hours away. A bunch of taxi drivers are pinned down too and are hanging around the bus station. If anyone knows how to get out of here, it will be them. I approach one of them, a guy in his late twenties. Crouched down, smoking a cigarette, he's chatting to the other cabbies.

'*Hola, amigo, que pasa?*' I ask. 'My friends and I would like to leave Pasto tonight,' I say, pointing to where Cillian, Mark and Tara are sitting.

He nods.

'I will tell you if that's possible, *amigo*,' he says.

After another hour, it becomes dark and we resign ourselves to a rough night's sleep in the bus terminal, without mattresses or sleeping bags.

'Aren't we glad we didn't cycle through this place? You feel it could explode at the drop of a pin,' says Cillian.

I have the same feeling. There's a sense that society in Colombia is capable of exploding in a way that just wouldn't occur back home.

'Must be about fifty riot police out there,' I say.

Suddenly, my taxi driver runs at full speed towards where we're sitting.

'You want to get out of here?' he says in a loud whisper.

We pick up our bags and run as fast as we can behind him. We throw our bags into the boot of the taxi and jump inside.

'How much?'

'*Mas tarde, mas tarde*,' he says. I guess we'll discuss that later.

In a squeal of tyres, we take off, following a convoy of about twelve other taxis.

'Ecuador?' the driver asks.

'Yes, Ecuador!' we cry.

At the other side of Pasto, all is calm. Signs of rioting on the streets are evident, but it seems things have died down for the time being. The police had given a ten-minute window for traffic to get through the town's centre and we hit the gap.

At a bus terminal just before the border, at Ipiales, the taxi drops us off.

'Thank you. You live in a very crazy country,' Cillian says to the taxi driver and pays over $30. The Londoners pay their own fare.

'*Si, loco*!' says the taxi man, laughing.

Mark checks his bags to make sure they haven't been used to smuggle anything over the border. We do the same. We shake hands with him and Tara and they take another taxi to the next town.

'It was brief, chaps, but I'm sure I'll never forget either of you. Good luck with the rest of it,' says Mark.

We'll be able to catch a bus to Quito in a couple of hours.

As we wait in the bus terminal in Ipiales, I wonder if I ever envisaged anything like today happening to me. My mind wanders back to the media campaign that promoted PACT right up to when we left Ireland and the image we presented. It seems, now, that that was all a different world and in relation to a different trip, as I imagined it.

We actively courted the media and promoted the journey at every opportunity available before we left: four young Irish lads take on the Pan-American Highway for charity. Our idea was that a strong media campaign would raise a lot of money for the charity by increasing awareness and encouraging more people to donate. If there was any form of publicity offered to us, we accepted it, immediately. D4hotels became PACT's official sponsor in June 2008, a little over two months before we left Ireland. Securing this sponsorship of €25,000 was Brian's brief and he pulled it off perfectly, harassing Sean Dunne's personal assistant, every day until the cheque was signed. D4hotels upped the ante in relation to the media coverage we received. They wanted a return for the €25,000 they had put up so they employed a professional PR company to maximise the trip's publicity. Interviews on radio shows, newspaper coverage and television appearances were secured. Briefly, PACT became quite a well-known organisation: lots of people knew what we were doing. We appeared on the Ray D'Arcy and Sean Moncrieff shows.

The culmination of our media campaign before we left Ireland was a slot on the *Saturday Night with Miriam* show, hosted by Miriam O'Callaghan. We appeared on the first night of the show's season after an interview with Red Hurley and Louis Walsh. Each of us was asked one question. The producer of the show rang us all a few days beforehand to confirm the answers to our questions. There was no confusion.

'So Ben, why bicycles?' asked Miriam.

I really wanted to say, 'I haven't a clue Miriam; it just sounds like a good idea' but I replied with the producer's line that the bicycles were a good compromise between doing the trip on foot or in a car.

I couldn't wait to get out of RTÉ. Appearing on national television, telling the country we were going to cycle from one end of the Americas to the other, made me feel uncomfortable. At that point, I still didn't own a bicycle and had yet to cycle any long distances on successive days. My total cycling experience at that point was a trip from Dublin to Trim and back. While on the show, we were wearing brand new, tight cycling jerseys complete with our sponsor's logo; a Sunday league pub soccer team would have looked in better shape. Worried about what people might think, I was embarrassed telling the whole country about our plans to cycle from Alaska to Argentina, when the truth was I had no idea about cycling.

Now I would have a few stories worth telling Miriam if her producers wouldn't mind me answering the questions myself.

PERU

4–8 December 2008

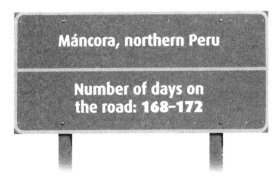

Máncora, northern Peru

Number of days on
the road: 168–172

Number of kilometres completed: **12,464**

After a month off, we're nearly back on the bikes. The support jeep and our bikes were shipped to Guayaquil, a port town midway down the Ecuadorian coastline. This is the location from which tourists, scientists and geographers begin expeditions to the Galapagos Islands. The islands are 972 km off the mainland, in the South Pacific. One can take a plane to the islands but, typically, people travel there by boat. The Galapagos are, of course, famous for their central role in Charles Darwin's theory of evolution and are home to a vast array of animals and plants. Guayaquil has prospered from the Galapagos connection and has a number of upmarket hotels, restaurants and shopping facilities.

Trying to release the container from the port proves

almost as difficult as getting it onto the boat in the first place. The authorities delay and delay until we pay even more money for fictitious bureaucratic procedures to be completed. At this stage we have handed over more than $2,000 to get this container moving. When the container is presented finally, we break the seal and are delighted to see everything is still in one piece; we were fearing things may have been damaged

Brian McDermott and Ben cycle uphill in the desert in northern Peru.

en route or, more likely, stolen. Everyone is delighted to get going again. You're either dying to get off the bike or can't wait to get back on it – a love-hate relationship.

We peddle out of Guayaquil with big smiles on our faces. Crossing large dangerous intersections, we find our way out of the city.

'South America, baby!' shouts Alan.

'Just ten thousand kilometres to go,' cries John, last in the group.

Flat roads out of the city will bring us all the way to the border with Peru through the Equadorian Lowlands. FWG are no longer with us. It's actually a bit of a relief and more enjoyable without the security guys following us. The climate is more comfortable than Central America: it's less humid and the heat is dry so we're not constantly soaking wet.

Our first night back on the road is spent in Narjaral, after which we continue towards Arinillas, a town near the Peruvian border. The flat road winds through vast banana plantations. Small planes fly overhead, dusting the crops with fertiliser. Long straight irrigation ditches run perpendicular to the road for kilometres into the distance. We haven't seen such intense cultivation since California.

At the bustling town of Huaquillas lies the border crossing between Ecuador and Peru. The kilometres on either side of the town are barren and sparse but Huaquillas is alive with street vendors, live music and milling crowds. Walking through the town with our bikes, we are the centre of attention. Locals harass us interminably to buy counterfeit sunglasses, clothes and electronics. The pace is frenetic and the noise from the street, immense.

We pass into Peru without incident and the road south runs directly alongside the Pacific coastline. All becomes deathly quiet once again. Peru is vast; the coastline measures 2,500 km to the Chilean border and Lima is almost exactly halfway down the coast. As we approach the Peruvian desert, we see the first signs of a harsher landscape. The Pacific is a constant to our right and scorched barren hills follow us on our left. On 6 December, we arrive at the town of Máncora and check ourselves into the Loki Hostel, which is a chain of three: the one here, one in Lima and another in Cusco. It's full of European backpackers, plenty of Irish too. A fantastic welcome awaits us. A table quiz is organised by the staff and the proceeds will be given to us for the charity.

After a quick shower, I head down to the bar, order a double whiskey and Coke and breathe a sigh of relief; no more cycling for a few days. Plonking myself at a table with a group of other guests, I introduce myself. Conversation immediately stops and everyone stares at me. The questioning begins. Where did you start? What was the best place you passed through? How many kilometres do you cover a day? Did you ever feel like giving up?

We're a novelty wherever we go. When we arrive in backpacker places like this, people don't want to talk about anything else.

'I'd love to do something like that but there's just no way I could,' says Kate, a girl in her late twenties from Cork.

'I suppose you don't know if you can or you can't do these things until you try,' I say.

It's strange the way people accept they've failed before they try to succeed. Some are baffled by the fact that we've cycled here from northern Alaska. Some think it's cool; others think it's daft.

'So you just pass through places? You don't spend any time actually in the places?'

But, for me, the enjoyable aspect of travelling isn't about place. It's about the travelling itself. The state of being transitory – of not being in one place or the other – is why I enjoy what we are doing. When we cycle for periods without seeing westerners, I forget that what we're doing actually is so unusual. The people of Central America and Mexico weren't bothered by us at all. Not once in Guatemala did I encounter any questions about the total distance of the journey or how long we cycle every week.

A sandy beach beside the hostel keeps us occupied for a few days and restaurants serve a local dish called civiche: fish cured in lime juice, which isn't too bad.

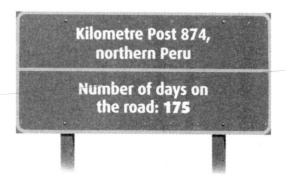

Kilometre Post 874, northern Peru

Number of days on the road: 175

Number of kilometres completed: **12,770**

We get going again and climb approximately 250 metres to a desert plateau. We're coming into the northern Peruvian desert or the 'Peruvian Sahara', as some books and websites call it. It's extremely windy and we're being hit dead on from the south. Progress is cut to a third of what it's normally like. Wind like this uproots trees. For this reason, the trip is normally completed from south to north. Touring expeditions coming the other way sail up the coast. We knew this when we organised the trip but we didn't realise the wind would be quite this strong; we've underestimated it. From Tallara, we make our way towards Piura covering 45 km in three hours; frustratingly slow progress. Disheartened, we're all clearly asking ourselves if it's going to be like this for the next three months.

'And we haven't even talked about how hard the Andes are going to be yet,' John says.

We're shocked at the force of the wind but it's not the only thing we're dealing with because it's extremely dry too. In Central America, the humidity coated us in a constant sweaty film but now the air sucks the moisture from our bodies, leaving our skin like sandpaper. With my index finger, I'm able to write my name on my forearm. My cycling gear is covered in patches of salt and the back of my throat is parched. About 8 kilometres from Piura, my toes cramp and I fall off the bike. In agony, my calves seize. I take on a litre of water, stretch and get going again, a few minutes behind the others.

We pass through populated areas that don't appear on any of our maps and come across scores of people living in shanty settlements. These communities have no names or the normal characteristics of towns or villages; there are no shops, paved streets or street lighting. The people here are anonymous to the rest of the world. From Piura, the map indicates that there's nothing for the next 220 km but we know this is not to say that we won't come across people. Cycling deeper into the desert, we're hoping we'll come across any sort of shelter because the wind is stronger now. Organising ourselves into train formation, we try to make things easier. Sand blows into our eyes. There's nothing on the horizon but sand dunes and open road. The wind howls loudly in our ears. No traffic passes by for hours. Sand blows on to the road, covering it totally in parts. About two hours before sunset, Neil comes back up the road with bad news.

'I've driven for an hour south and there's nothing; looks like we're on the sand tonight, lads,' he says.

We agree to keep on going until we find a place to pitch the tents and prepare food. At Kilometre Post 874, we come across a low enclosure made from brick: a sheep pen or the remains of a house. There's a large pile of rubbish, including some sticks, inside it, which we can burn. We pitch the two tents on the outside of the northerly pen wall, giving ourselves the best possible protection from the wind or the 'animal', as we've renamed it, which continues to roar from the south. Not long after the fire is lit, the last of the daylight disappears and a full moon emerges. Simultaneously, like a switch being flicked off, the wind disappears and the desert becomes deathly still.

As I eat, I can't help thinking we're doing things the wrong way round. Why are we cycling during the day when the wind is at its strongest? I look around and everyone is shattered. To complete the same distances, we must be exerting at least double the effort.

'Why don't we cycle at night and rest up during the day?' I say to the group, anticipating a reluctant response.

Silence.

'With these flat roads and with no wind we'd hammer out 130 kilometres in five hours; 3 a.m. to 8 a.m. What do you reckon?'

'There's no wind now but that doesn't mean there'll be no wind right throughout the night,' says John.

'It's been like this since we've been here; once the temperature drops, the wind disappears. The wind is generated by heat,' I counter.

'It's too dangerous, Benjy. Cycling in the pitch dark on these roads? I just think it's too risky,' says Alan.

'Well, we have to do something. We can't keep on doing

ten hours a day in these conditions. We have to start getting up much earlier.'

If we get up at 3 a.m. or 4 a.m. and get four hours done before sunrise, it will take the pressure off.

'Do we want to keep cycling in this wind?' I ask.

I'm shocked by the lack of interest in the idea. Why not change the plan? Why don't we give it a try at least?

Because it takes so long from the time we wake up every morning to the time we leave, I reckon if we get up at 4 a.m. we could be on the road by 5.30 a.m., giving ourselves approximately two hours of cycling without wind. This will amount to 50 completed kilometres. Everyone reluctantly agrees we should try it.

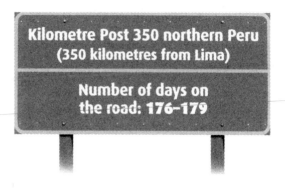

Kilometre Post 350 northern Peru
(350 kilometres from Lima)

Number of days on
the road: 176–179

Number of kilometres completed: **13,194**

I wake up at 4 a.m. and attempt to get the ball rolling. Alan is straight out of the tent too but it's hard to get the rest of the lads in gear quickly.

'Let's beat the wind, lads, come on, let's go!' I shout.

By the time we're packed up and ready to go, it's 6 a.m. For three windless hours, we cycle, the first hour and a half of which is completed in the dark. We coast along effortlessly. As dawn rises, the desert dunes light up like scoops of caramel ice cream. The collective whir of the bikes' wheels in the still dawn is music to my ears. Just as the switch turned off last night, it turns back on at about 10 a.m. and the wind pummels us for the rest of the day. Ten kilometres from the town of Chiclayo, Cillian falls sick, so we pull in. After the fast progress this morning, there's less objection to an early start tomorrow.

Chiclayo, 770 km from Lima, is one of Peru's showcase towns and the most developed we've been to in the north of Peru by a longshot. After we check into a hotel, we stroll down the town. We pass a nursing college, language schools and dozens of bars and restaurants. Students and young professionals pass us by. It's a world apart from the people of the desert.

We are about halfway into Peru before I realise how big it is. The country's coastline is approximately the same length as that of the west coast of the United States. I didn't realise that half of the country is a vast desert expanse or appreciate just how harsh the climate is here. I don't think any of us really knew much about Peru before we got here. Looking east into the desert, you see nothing but rolling sand dunes and this is without considering the mountainous territory of the Andes to the east where the famous site of Machu Pichu is located. Cycling for hours we see no people, towns or traffic. Other than a small number of industries located on the outskirts of Chiclayo, there has been little other sign of commercial activity. Absence of soil, water and shelter means most of the region is not a suitable place to rear crops or keep animals. The desert of northern Peru is not a place where humans can easily live.

Early morning starts mean faster progress and the collective attitude of the group is beginning to accept this fact. On 14 December, our early morning cycling takes us from the desert to an irrigated valley where green fields and trees abruptly replace sand dunes and unsheltered wind. Suddenly, people are walking along the sides of the road and out working in green fields. Women carrying bundles of

Smiling children sit for a photo at a desert village in the Peruvian desert.

sticks strapped to their backs walk in single file against us. After completing 100 km for the day, we decide we deserve a night out of the desert. At a small factory with a grassy area outside it, we pull in to see about pitching the tents, but a security guard stationed outside says we must move on.

Myself and Neil jump into the jeep and drive 200 metres back up the road, looking for another suitable place. We see a small farm house.

'Right, pull in here, I'll ask,' I say.

After knocking on the door and realising no one was at home, we walk around behind the house to the farmyard. Two donkeys are tied to a fence and dogs and chickens scurry around. A man, out in the fields, puts down his scythe and walks towards us. I wave to him.

'*Hola Señor,*' I call.

'*Hola Señors,*' he says as he approaches us.

'*Mi nombre is Ben y este es mi amigo, Neil. Seria possible acampar en su jardin por la noche?*' I say, giving my name and Neil's and asking for permission to camp in his garden for the night.

'*Si, si amigos … qui mis invitados!* says Lucion, agreeing to be our host for the evening.

'*Muchas gracias,*' Neil and I say together.

By the time we tell the lads what's going on, get back to the farmyard and start pitching the tents, Lucion has brought his cows in from the field and has began milking them. Four cows in total, they are being milked one at a time. The cows wait patiently in line while he sits on a small stool and attaches a mechanical milking device to each animal in turn. Alan offer a helping hand and slips seamlessly back into the work of the dairy farmer. Lucion says he sells his milk to Nestlé but struggles to survive on the prices they pay him.

We take off the next morning at 5 a.m. in total darkness. It must nearly be milking time again. A thick mist covers the fields. The desert is just about to wake up. We peddle approximately 200 metres from the farmyard when I look back and see Lucion waving us good bye, a flashlight in his hand. He continues to wave until we're almost out of sight. The light from his flashlight gradually fades in the darkness.

It's not long before we're back in the desert, struggling against the wind again. We have lunch in Chipoté and then stop later in the day in Casma. We get as far as Kilometre Post 350 (350 kilometres from Lima) at which point we meet Neil in the support jeep.

'No towns for at least 100 kilometres. But there's a restaurant up the road a bit. Maybe we can stay there?' he says.

The restaurant is closed for the night. Myself, Alan and Brian walk around the side to the entrance of the private residence. Before one of us knocks on the door, a small elderly man wearing big thick spectacles comes out.

'*Hola*. My name Clemente,' he says, in broken English.

Clemente walks us towards a building beside his house and gestures for us to follow him. He leads us inside and shows us a number of rooms with two or three beds in each.

'My friends, please rest here tonight. The shower room is just down the corridor,' says Clemente.

'And how much do we owe you for this?' Alan asks.

Clemente doesn't answer, instead he says that we should come inside for food when we're ready.

Fish and chips are prepared for dinner and a large pot of hot coffee is placed on the table. Clemente doesn't speak much English but we're able to tell him the basics about our trip so far. Many travellers have passed by here in the past, he says. A large scrapbook is produced in which dozens of travellers have written, detailing their journeys. Like ourselves, they had all been taken in by Clemente when they found themselves stranded in the desert and in need of a bed. Flicking through the book and the most notable of all inscriptions is that of Karl Bushby, the man we narrowly missed meeting in Fairbanks. Bushby writes:

'I was tired and hungry and then I came across this

place. Be nice to this man [Clemente]. He renewed my faith in humanity at a time I needed it most.'

I then write in the book:

'To our friend Clemente: thank you for your kindness. It is a pleasure to read all the wonderful comments by other travellers and be part of Pan-American Highway history. Safe travels.'

I ask Clemente to write a note in my diary and he writes the following:

'*Estas liueas sou para mi amigo* Ben *que uego aqui con el grupo de amigos Izfou deses que recorrou el euizido en busca de ayuda para los ninos de Africa. Todos per admirable. Tu amigo siempre,* Clemente.'

'To my friend Ben who with his friends are collecting money for the children of Africa. All very admirable. Your friend always, Clemente.'

Clemente offers us more to eat and he deals with each of us with warmly. A genuinely good man – a stranger – and I see where Bushby is coming from. A smile never leaves his face. He understands why we're travelling. We sit around the table with smiles on our faces too.

Maybe the wind isn't such a big deal? Maybe all our problems aren't that important after all?

Barranca

Number of days on
the road: **180**

Number of kilometres completed: **13,669**

This time last year we were at home, finishing up in college and getting ready for a cold Christmas. This year, we've arranged to spend Christmas on the beach. Brian and Neil's parents are flying out from Ireland for a week to be with us. A villa has been booked at a place called Playa Bonita, about 100 km south of Lima. We'll take five or six days off. Everyone is really looking forward to the break.

But, for now, the battle against the desert continues. Leaving Clemente's home, we take off: the sixth day of cycling in a row.

'Be safe Irish men,' says Clemente.

Clemente won't accept any money for what he provided for us so we leave $100 on a bedside locker; less than a hotel and a meal would have cost for the group. Not long into the day, during a short break, John looks extremely pale and it's clear he's not feeling well. He's not one to point it out himself or admit that he can't go on and we have to convince him he's not fit enough to continue.

'I'm grand, lads. After a few minutes and some water I'll be fine,' says John.

Thirty-five kilometres north of Barranca – approximately 370 km north of Lima – we stop and eat lunch, in silence. John falls asleep. While we sit facing the road, thinking of the best way to manage the situation, a convoy of half a dozen circus vehicles passes by, going north. A caged vehicle containing four tigers and a trailer with an elephant go past.

'See nothing for a day and then you can't believe your eyes,' Alan says.

'So Johnny, what's the story? I think you'll have to ride shotgun with Neil for the rest of the day. We'll have to kick on,' says Alan.

John doesn't say anything: he just gets to his feet, walks straight over to the jeep, gets inside and falls asleep. Brian puts John's bike in the trailer and progress continues. I know how he feels; the idea of not cycling even a small fraction of this journey is something we all dislike. When we get home and someone asks 'Did you cycle the whole length of the road?', we would all like to say, yes. Even though 30 km is an insignificant distance, you'd rather be on the bike than in the jeep.

When we arrive in Barranca, Neil has booked a few rooms in a hotel and John is already in bed. Barranca is quite a busy town. Tuk-tuk taxis dart around. There are no other westerners in sight. Stalls selling rip-off designer sun glasses and clothes clutter the streets. A half chicken, chips and a coke costs 15 soles; about €2. Neil drives on to Lima to collect his two sisters, Aisling and Louise, and Brian's girlfriend, Shauna, all of whom are also coming out for Christmas. At the moment, the plan is to get closer to Lima tomorrow, but we'll have to see how John feels in the morning.

19–21 December 2008

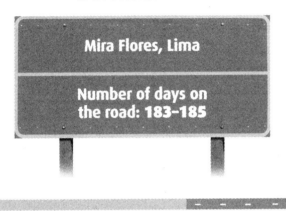

Mira Flores, Lima

Number of days on
the road: 183–185

Number of kilometres completed: **13,871**

We're up at 3.15 a.m. and on the road by 4.15 a.m. It has taken John two days to recover: food poisoning, I'd say. The roads are quiet and unlit, our last day of cycling before Christmas. Coasting along in the dark, about 10 km out from Barranca, Rob hits a rock, which sends him flying over the handlebars. A collective squeal of brakes: progress grinds to a halt. Initially, he remains on the ground, moving very little. Alan picks Rob's bike up off the road. The rest of us see if he's OK.

'Never saw it,' Rob says.

The distance between the bike and where Rob now sits on the road is at least 5 metres.

'Everything feel all right?' asks Brian.

'Yeah, just a bit shocked, I think. C'mon, let's get into Lima,' says Rob.

I know Rob would have to be very seriously hurt for things to stop. A couple of years ago, after falling off his bike in Laos, he broke his leg and had to be airlifted to Bangkok for surgery.

By 12 noon, we've completed 160 km, without doubt the fastest progress on the road so far. My front derailleur, the mechanism that changes gears up and down at the front of the bike, snaps. Without it working properly I have to stop the bike and manually lift the chain up or down depending on whether I'm going up- or downhill. With a number of tough climbs coming into Lima, I have to stop regularly and move the chain down to the easiest gear, and then get going again.

Coming into Lima is dangerous. A four-lane highway with a number of underpasses means our concentration has to be 100 per cent. Weaving in and out of traffic is dangerous but also enjoyable and brings a rush of adrenalin. As we get closer to the city centre and traffic intensifies, I look back and see Cillan with earphones in, listening to his iPod. With several lanes of traffic, as well as merging traffic and cars overtaking at high speeds, this looks like utter suicide.

'Cillers, for f*** sake, take the earphones out,' shouts Brian back to him.

Cillian doesn't hear anything and continues on towards the city. When we come off the main road and things quieten down, we stop to take the map out and see about getting to Mira Flores, the area where we're staying.

'You lunatic, that's suicide,' says Alan to Cillian.

'I knew what I was doing. Look after yourself and I'll do the same, all right?' says Cillian.

Things can get a bit tetchy on the last day of a week. All of us can't wait to stop cycling for Christmas.

With a population of over 7 million people, Lima is a very large, very densely crowded city. We pass sprawling slums but relatively wealthy middle class areas too. The city is busy and booming. In 2006, the Peruvian stock exchange was the most profitable in the world. The unemployment rate in the city stands at a little over 7.2 per cent, half that of many European countries. The main commodities exports, leaving the country via Lima, are oil, steel, silver, zinc, cotton, sugar and coffee. The slums on the city's periphery are a sharp contrast to the clean streets and colonial architecture of the centre – a different country to the territory we've just come through.

Brian and Neil's parents, Niall and Deirdre, are staying in a hotel a few kilometres from Mira Flores. It's been three months and about 10,000 km since we last saw Niall in San Diego.

'It's hard to believe you've been cycling all this time since San Diego,' says Niall.

'I have half a suitcase full of rashers and sausages for breakfasts over Christmas. We're going to recharge your batteries so you can get to the end of the road,' Deirdre says.

Strangely, it's the first time someone has mentioned the end or alluded about the inevitability of the trip finishing. As far as we're concerned, it's still a long way off. But I suppose it isn't really. After Christmas, we'll be entering into our last push. Only two more countries left to cycle through. Only two more months left.

Number of kilometres completed: **13,971**

On 22 December, we cycle 100 km south of Lima to Playa Bonita, where Niall and Deirdre have rented a villa for Christmas. Located right beside the beach and with a roof-top area with sunloungers and a barbeque, it's the perfect place for the next few days. Beside the villa development is a tacky, modern shopping complex, with a cinema and restaurants, that sticks out from the surrounding environment. The local town itself is more like the Peru we know and myself, Niall and Alan head into the markets to pick up supplies.

It's 27 °C on Christmas Day – moderately hot by our standards. First thing in the morning, I take a swim in the sea and then we all kick a football around on the beach. A meal and a few beers are followed by a sing-song later in the evening.

27–31 December 2008

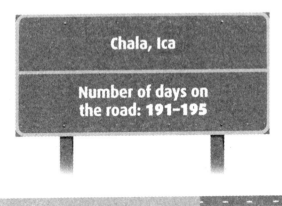

Chala, Ica

Number of days on the road: 191–195

Number of kilometres completed: **14,614**

Unlike at home, where Christmas can drag on for days, our break ends on 27 December when we get going again. We move out of the villa and into a hotel a few kilometres down the road. The time off has given us the opportunity to get into good mental and physical shape so that we can take on the rest of the trip. Without Niall and Deirdre coming over, I don't think we would have done much, if anything at all, for Christmas. Niall and Deirdre head off to Cusco to visit Machu Pichu before they go home. We get back on the road.

Paddy and Conor, two UCD students, come out from Ireland. Paddy is the son of Kieran O'Connor and Conor is Brian's first cousin. The lads plan on spending a few weeks with us before they'll have to return for the next semester in

UCD. Neil collects them from the airport. They arrive at the hotel in the middle of the night and go straight to bed.

On the morning of the 28th we get up early, make a few small repairs to bikes and attempt to get back on the road. Deirdre brought over a new derailleur from Ireland and I fix it to my bike. Paddy and Conor, thrown straight into the thick of things, are like rabbits in headlights. We all briefly say hello to one another but there's stuff to be done and kilometres to be completed.

'Hi lads, Happy Christmas, you're very welcome to the group. Are you both ready to go?' asks Cillian.

A couple of days ago, both of these newcomers were in Dublin, eating Christmas turkey. Now they're getting ready to cycle into the Atacama Desert where it's 30 °C and very dry. Later, when things settle down, Conor tells me that people back home are following our progress on the website and reading my articles in *The Irish Times*.

South of Lima, the landscape is less extreme and the desert becomes much flatter, not like the rolling dunes of the north. On 30 December, we cycle towards the village of Nazca and through the famous Nazca Lines, which are etched onto the desert, about 25 km north of the town. At the side of the road is a high tower where passers-by can climb up and view the lines, which are a series of ancient geolyphs. The area encompassing the lines is an enormous 500 square kilometres. There are hundreds of individual figures, including humming-birds, spiders, monkeys, fish, sharks, llamas and lizards. Typically, they are about 200 metres in length. Small planes on sightseeing expeditions drone overhead in the cloudless sky. From the top of the viewing tower, you can just about make out the figure of a monkey and a tree. The Nazca Lines were declared a UNESCO world heritage site in 1994 and our road goes right through the region.

Dropping back down to the coast, the wind intensifies. After lunch, we cycle parallel to the Pacific. Sand blows onto the road and covers it entirely for large stretches as a bulldozer pushes the sand back towards the coast, allowing traffic to pass. At one point, the thickness of the sand forces us to dismount and walk with our bikes. As quickly as a tract of sand is cleared, the wind blows a fresh layer over it again. Sand blows into our faces constantly.

At the end of the day, New Year's Eve, we arrive in the town of Chala and decide to treat the evening like any other. Deciding to take an early night and not go out and celebrate, we agree that, in the greater scheme of things, it would be better to keep momentum up tomorrow. The town is getting ready to celebrate; stages are being erected and people are out on the streets drinking bottles of beer. But, after a meal of fried chicken and chips, we all take an early night.

At midnight I'm woken by loud banging and fireworks, which I swear could be going off in the bathroom down the corridor. A band, directly outside the hotel, starts playing and drunk Peruvians roar along, singing. Not able to sleep, I lie in bed, staring directly up at the ceiling. Bright flashes illuminate the bedroom. Happy New Year, I think; seven months on the road.

1 January 2009

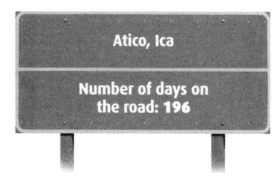

Atico, Ica

Number of days on
the road: 196

Number of kilometres completed: **14,699**

We're up and ready to go at 8 a.m. I have a fantastic premonition for the New Year, a feeling of achievement. Normally, in the past, the New Year meant little to me but now it seems significant. The band outside the hotel plays on and drunken youngsters are still outside, hanging around the streets.

'Happy New Year, lads. What's our distance today?' says Alan, keen to concentrate on the main objective.

We spin out of the town and climb back, away from the coast, onto the desert again. Halfway through the day, I hear retching and look around to see Alan, hunched over his bike. Outside a restaurant in the small fishing village of Atico, Alan vomits repeatedly and then lies out on the floor of the restaurant, sweating profusely. After a quick glance at one another myself and Brian decide to call it a day and, against Alan's protestations, insist he goes to bed to sleep it off.

CHILE

2–7 January 2009

Arica, Chile

Number of days on
the road: 197–202

Number of kilometres completed: **15,346**

A friend from college, Ben Leonard Kane, is flying out to the desert to meet us and our itinerary for the next few days is determined by this. We're getting closer to Chile and we'll soon be leaving one desert and entering another: Chile's Atacama. I've heard it's an even tougher terrain than here but I have also learned to be suspicious of what people say about the Pan-American Highway.

We arrive at the seaside town of Camana, approximately 580 km from the Chilean border. Camana is the capital city of the Camana Province and is a popular holiday spot for local Peruvians, particularly those from the nearby larger city of Arequipa. It is a fine place for us to stop and wait for new arrivals and for anyone who's sick to recover.

Ben is flying into Arequipa tomorrow, so we debate whether we should carry on to meet him or take a rest day and collect him with the support jeep instead. When we discover that Arequipa is 160 km inland, with massive amounts of climbing, the decision to collect Ben in the jeep becomes an easy one. We'll have to cycle the same road on the way south anyway but not all the way to Arequipa. A turn-off, just before the city, will bring us back to the coast and very near to the border with Chile.

On 3 January, Rob and I collect Ben in the Jeep and bring him back to Camana. Ben, who made a late decision to come out and join us, is a travelling enthusiast. He and I have already backpacked around Australia together. He's worked and travelled in Africa and India, so I wasn't surprised when he said he'd like to come out to join us. Driving back down the steep roads to the coast I see he's worried at the prospect of cycling back up.

'How am I going to cycle up this?' he asks.

'Just don't think about it. After three days, you'll be at our pace, no problem,' I reassure him.

Two friends of Neil's, Jim and Paul, who caught a bus down from Lima, have also come out to join the group in recent days. Including support team and cyclists we're now fifteen people, our largest number since California. A quiet and enthusiastic guy, Jim was in catering college with Neil and will help with the cooking and the support effort generally. Paul is a friend of Jim's. Interested in cycling, he heard about the trip through Jim and was keen to get involved. Paul is going to travel in the support jeep most days but plans on cycling one of the spare bikes from time to time. Neither is interested in cycling every day.

On the morning of 4 January, I set out early with Ben

and Jim because they're worried they'll quickly fall behind. Cycling beside Ben, I talk him through gear changes, pace and other helpful techniques I learned myself over the past months. After thirty minutes or so the gradient of the road becomes a good deal steeper and the pace reduces to a slow climb.

'Get yourself into a gear you feel comfortable in, sit upright on the bike and just get into a good steady rhythm,' I tell the two lads.

Things go well for the next hour but soon Jim falls off the pace and, exhausted, gets off the bike to wait for the support jeep. Ben continues for another while but is forced off before we reach the top. I feel sorry for both; I know exactly what they're going through.

After half an hour Ben reaches the top of the climb, and things level out. At that point, the rest of the group catches up and together we spin quickly along flat ground to the turn-off crossroads before Arequipa. We pass through the green pastureland surrounding the village of El Alto, a town known for its dairy produce. Green fields on both sides of the road are full of cows. A local shop sells a variety of dairy products. Farm machinery rattles up and down the village.

From El Alto, the road drops quickly back to the coast, moving in and out of bays and headlands. Drops of 500 metres are followed immediately by climbs of 500 metres. It can take more than half an hour to climb 500 metres but only a few minutes to drop down the same distance. Long stretches of arid desert are broken by smaller green areas of intensive agriculture and sophisticated irrigation networks. On 5 and 6 January, we cycle big days – 195 km and 185 km respectively. This hard work and direct progress brings us to the town of Tacna, 35 km from the border with Chile. Ben, Jim and Paul are doing well and the last few days of hard cycling have brought them up to speed.

Tacna, our last stop in Peru, has a history of and reputation for national patriotism. Territory here, between Chile and Peru, has long been disputed. Many of the streets, monuments and statues in the city are named after Peruvian heroes who fought for the country's independence (1821–1824) and then in the War of the Pacific, in which Chile fought against Bolivia and Peru (1879–1883). Now, Tacna is a busy, commercial area, benefiting from being part of a duty-free zone and its close proximity to Chile. As we cycle the short distance to the Chilean border we pass a number of large supermarkets in which people from both countries are shopping. Cars pass by us, their boots laden with televisions, refrigerators and washing machines. There is no town at the border, just passport control buildings on either side, about 200 metres apart.

We cross over without hassle. After today, we will have only one more national border to cross. We're now on a road called the C5 that runs the entire length of Chile. The difference with Peru is stark. A more modern and European atmosphere is apparent here; people are better dressed, cars are newer and more expensive and the streets and roads are cleaner. About 20 km south of the border we arrive in Arica. Known as the City of the Eternal Spring, Arica was originally part of Peru but was won by Chile in the aftermath of the War of the Pacific. The clocks move forward two hours, so it's 9 p.m., rather than 7 p.m., when we arrive.

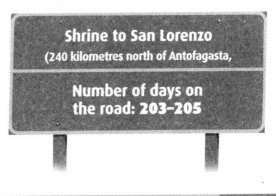

Shrine to San Lorenzo
(240 kilometres north of Antofagasta,

**Number of days on
the road: 203–205**

Number of kilometres completed: **15,826**

From Arica we begin the climb into the Chilean Atacama, a plateau on the Pacific coast, west of the Andes. The desert is, according to National Geographic and NASA, the driest place on Earth. Occupying 105,000 square kilometres in northern Chile (almost one and a half times the size of Ireland), it is composed of salt basins, sand and a red, burnt coloured substance called felsic lava. The average rainfall in the Chilean region of Antofagasta, in the Atacama, is one millimetre per year. Some weather stations in Atacama have never recorded rain. The Atacama has been used by film crews as a location for filming Mars scenes in films, most notably in the series, *Space Odyssey*. NASA has used the desert to test instruments for Mars expeditions. The Atacama is sparsely populated with most cities located along the Pacific coastline, typically 1,000 metres below the desert plateau.

We climb to 600 metres, then drop into a valley before climbing back to 1,200 metres. The colours of the desert are a mix of reds, browns, pinks and oranges. There's no sign of animals, soil or vegetation; the desert appears fantastically absent of life. The terrain is lacerated and scarred into giant valleys, canyons and ravines, with giant bare and pink glowing mountains providing a backdrop. This is more intense topography than we met in Peru.

The sides of the canyons are steep, falling straight down to flat valley floors, hundreds of metres below. The road twists and turns gradually, winding down the edge of the valley. Any mistakes will be fatal. The colours of the sides of the valley change constantly, depending on our height in relation to them and the brightness of the sunshine.

Just before lunch, we drop to approximately 300 metres. The road adopts a flat course, moving through the valleys for the next couple of hours. The valley's walls, on both sides of the road, tower high above us. Thousands of boulders, varying between the size of footballs and small cars, are littered between us and the valley walls, making us feel even smaller still. Climbing upwards again, the group is quiet, appreciating the power of the environment, the most surreal place we have been yet.

The Atacama continues: desolate, uninhabited and barren. Mornings are cold and it only starts getting warmer from 10 a.m. On 9 January, we cycle 180 km, arriving in the middle of the desert at the end of the day. A miner's camp, Piradus, is located 100 metres down a steep embankment. We set up camp behind one of the pre-fabs and the workers allow us use their showers. A dozen bunk beds to a prefab, the miners are crammed into tight living spaces. Pictures of naked women line the walls of the living quarters and most of the men are lying on their beds, watching football on television. Bobby, a miner I chat with, has decent English. He says the desert has rich deposits of copper and other minerals and the world's largest supply of sodium nitrate, which was mined on a large scale until the 1940s. The desert is now littered with abandoned sodium nitrate mines because synthetic nitrate was invented in Germany in the 1940s. We've seen signs of these abandoned mines along the way. The main minerals mined these days are iron-ore and copper, Bobby says. The border dispute – the war – between Peru and Chile in the nineteenth century, so proudly memorialised back in Tacna, was about the control of these minerals, he says.

The average distances we've been covering every day have been vast – 170 km days are now the norm and it is showing in our levels of fitness. When there are no towns or places to stop in, we may as well keep on going and get ahead of schedule, creating time off for ourselves farther down the road. After cycling 170 km in a day, you realise that it isn't all that difficult, so the inclination is to go at least that distance again the next day. Cycling big distances makes you want to cycle even bigger distances. We need to stop only to rest and eat; the landscape can be appreciated best from the saddle of the bike.

Another 160 km brings us to a roadside restaurant. We camp in a gazebo, beside a shrine to the martyr San Lorenzo. A family, who spent last night camping here and who are now leaving, offer us a collection of cold soft drinks, which we share among ourselves. To the left of the shrine, behind a few bushes, using buckets of water, we wash ourselves down in full view of the occasional passing truck.

With the build up of salt and sweat over the course of a day it is vital to wash down after cycling. If you fail to keep clean, rashes and sores on your legs and backside can flare up quickly.

'Antofagasta is 240 kilometres away. I reckon we can make that tomorrow,' I say to the group as we sit around eating.

'Yeah, why not?' Brian says.

'It means we'll have to leave first thing and take only short breaks. There can't be any messing around; if we want to make it there tomorrow we have to smash it all day long,' I say.

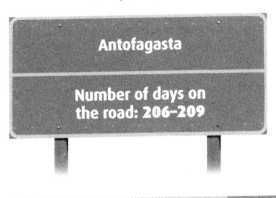

Number of kilometres completed: **16,060**

I jump out of the tent at 6 a.m. with the sole focus of reaching Antofagasta. I know now from the last months of experience, that if we want to cycle 240 km before sunset, we must leave early and cycle hard all day. If we do that, then we'll have a chance but 240 km is an extremely long distance to cycle in one day – it's the same distance as from Dublin to Westport.

Rob and I are ready before everyone else. Let's go! For me, the 240 km to Antofagasta represents a challenge within a challenge. I want to see if I can cycle 240 km; I want to push the farthest daily distance out again. I don't feel the same enthusiasm within the group.

Rob and I take off, stopping only for short regular breaks. Our pace is fast and things move along quickly enough to put Antofagasta within reach. Later in the day, after lunch, the support jeep catches up with us. Neil drives beside us and rolls his window down.

'Lads, you're 60 kilometres ahead of everyone else. They're breaking for too long,' says Neil.

'Well, what do we do?' says Rob

'That's up to you,' says Neil.

'Do you think they'll make it in to Antofagasta?' I ask Neil.

'I don't know. You lads keep going. Don't hang around waiting,' says Neil.

Rob and I take some water from the jeep, have a quick sandwich and get going again. Neil and the crew wait by the side of the road for the rest of the lads to catch up. Working hard and breaking the headwind for each other, we make fast progress and arrive at a small village 35 km north of Antofagasta at around 6 p.m. An ice cream van is parked outside a petrol station on the northern edge of the small settlement. With dry throats, and covered in sand and dust, we sit by the side of the road licking our ice cream cones.

'I feel bad about going on ahead, maybe we should have waited?' Rob says.

'Yeah, maybe we should have but we're here now, so we might as well keep going,' I say.

We drop rapidly to the coast, into Antofagasta. The town is the capital of the Antofagasta region and the first real city we've come across in northern Chile. Situated by a large bay, and with a port, we see a large urban centre as we drop ever faster towards it. A mining city, it is the hub of the surrounding mining area. Dump trucks and other heavy machinery storm by. As we've seen along the road, the surrounding area's development is based mainly on copper mining but also on other minerals such as nitrate and iodine, all of which have sustained Antofagasta's growth. Antofagasta PLC, a large company that is traded in London, owns and operates three copper mines in the region and is the principal provider of cargo transport and water distribution in the Antofagasta region. It's annual production of copper amounts to almost 700,000 tonnes. This part of northern Chile seems to be booming.

We check into a hotel, order a takeaway McDonald's and wait at the main square of the town for the rest of the group.

'They definitely didn't make it,' says Rob at 9 p.m. when there's still no sign of the support jeep or of anyone else. We turn in for the night.

The end of the road is now very much in sight. Days of cycling long distances are passing quickly and in a blur. Days are rolling into each other and weeks are passing by in a flash. More regularly, I'm thinking of home and the aftermath of the trip. What am I going to do when I go home? Would I like to jump straight into another expedition? What do I want to do with the rest of my life?

The fear of not reaching the end of the road no longer exists. Apart from a disaster – baring death – we now know we'll finish. Looking at the calendar, the rest of the journey appears manageable and, sticking to the plan, we should finish ahead of schedule. My parents are flying out to meet us in Argentina. We're planning to meet them in Mendoza, Argentina, just over the Andes, in around two weeks' time. My own focus now is to get there on schedule and spend some time with them for a few days. I plan on taking some time away from the rest of the group.

The next morning the rest of the group arrive into Antofagasta. I send Brian an email to let them know the name of the hotel where Rob and I are staying. I can tell the lads are slightly irate that we went on ahead of them yesterday but things aren't too serious.

'What happened to you?' I ask Brian and Alan.

'Pulled up a hundred kilometres short; it was just the way things worked out,' says Brian.

'You must have hammered it unbelievably hard,' says Alan.

'I'm sorry; we were just so far ahead that we thought we should keep going,' I say

'No problem, Benny, but just remember we're a team. We go at the last man's pace,' says Alan.

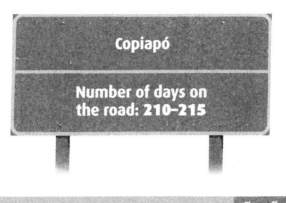

Copiapó

Number of days on the road: 210–215

Number of kilometres completed: **16,569**

On the morning of 15 January, we move out of Antofagasta. Three full days have been spent, eating, sleeping and generally not straying very far from the hotel. I'd like to say we explored the whole town but we didn't. I'd like to say we visited museums and went sightseeing but we didn't. I slept for endless hours. Brian conducted a radio interview with 98FM and I filed my latest piece for *The Irish Times*. I took my bike to a local shop and had it serviced and the brake pads replaced.

Now 1,300 km from our turn-off point, I appreciate just how long Chile is; approximately 5,000 km. Ruta 5 is the longest highway in Chile and will take us all the way to our turn-off point to Argentina, 80 km north of Santiago. The climb back up from the coast is hellishly long and brings us to the brutal desert where the wind, sand and emptiness waits for us. The road resumes its due south direction and the show goes on. The wind gusts. Quiet progress is interrupted by violent bursts that blow us to the very side of the road, often threatening to knock us off onto the sand.

The Atacama continues to be as severe as before. Any change in the landscape will be a huge contrast. The paradox of the desert is that, although it seems to be so absent of life, it makes you feel incredibly alive. This is a part of the world that has been stripped bare to the bone.

On 18 January, 280 km south of Antofagasta, we stop for lunch at Copiapó. The countryside is irrigated, green and fertile, and the difference takes us by surprise. It seems like we've left the Atacama for good but the maps aren't clear and some of the group, like John, doubt it. We have not encountered a sign along the road stating that we have officially left Atacama.

Vines and olives grow more regularly and people at small wooden stalls are selling watermelons and fruit juices. Thick with the smell of herbs, the scent in the air makes the cycling much more enjoyable. At Copiapó, we discover that the Dakar Rally has just passed through the area. Usually a race from France to Dakar, Senegal, it has moved to Chile and Peru for this year. Running parallel to the main road, a dirt track has been following us for hundreds of kilometres. We camped on the road last night, not knowing exactly what it was for.

'You crazy,' says the waitress in the restaurant. 'Big trucks and cars drive over those roads – all day and night,' she continues.

'Where is the race now?' I ask her.

'North; deep in the desert. Pass by four days ago.' she says.

'We would have seen the headlights and got off the road anyway,' says Cillian.

'You would have seen *nada*,' the woman insists.

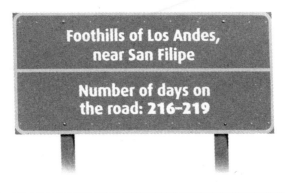

Foothills of Los Andes, near San Filipe

Number of days on the road: 216–219

Number of kilometres completed: **17,362**

'The Big Left Turn' is what we're calling the crossing of the Andes, from Chile into Argentina. It will take us two days to get up and over the highest point (approximately 3,000 metres). Two days of uphill climbing. The road in Chile has been relatively flat and, coming fully out of the Atacama, not particularly challenging or interesting. Climbing over the Andes represents a serious challenge and will be the longest continuous period of up hill cycling on the trip. Minds are focused and the group is approaching the Andes with caution, appreciating how difficult the route may be.

As we continue down Ruta 5, the Pacific lies to the west and the snow-capped Andes, in the distance, follow us to the east. From the bike, cycling alongside Brian, I gaze at the continuous row of mountains, getting ready for what's ahead. They look daunting.

'I presume the road will have to take a gradual course through the mountains?' I say, looking for reassurance.

'Yeah, it's the major commercial route between the two countries. I can't imagine the gradient will be too severe. But that just means the climbing will be more gradual and drawn out – I hope!' Brian says.

Approaching Santiago, the landscape becomes both more irrigated and populated. There are masses of fruit in the fields and the landscape is soft and forgiving. I'm reminded of California. Men and women wave white tassels, attempting to catch the attention of passing traffic to sell fruit, bread and cold drinks. It's great for us; refreshments are never very far away.

Eighty kilometres north of Santiago, we turn left and begin cycling due east. Late that evening, with the sun on our backs, we follow signposts for Los Andes and San Filipe; these towns are on the way up to the border with Argentina. About 30 km from where the road will start to rise more sharply, we stop at a petrol station for the night and pitch the tents on a grassy area behind the main building.

Truckers filling their tanks stare over at our encampment and chuckle.

25 January 2009

Guardia Vieja, Rio Blanco

Number of days on the road: 220

Number of kilometres completed: **17,412**

We cycle towards the Andes and it's like cycling towards a dark wall. As the mountains bear down on us, they become increasingly more intimidating. But the climb towards the town of Los Andes (850 metres) is gradual and pleasant with tree-lined roads and acres of vines groaning heavily with thick bunches of grapes. The Aconcagua Valley is one of the major wine regions of Chile. Cabernet Sauvignon is the main grape grown but the valley also produces Merlot and Syrah. A decent bottle of red costs very little in the local shops; cheaper than bottled water in some places.

Following the Aconcagua River, we climb, against its flow, all day. A solo cyclist, fully loaded with his gear and with a Japanese flag flying from the back of his bike, freewheels down and waves as he passes.

'I wonder is he on his way to Alaska,' I ask Cillian.

'Tell him to turn back. It's not worth it. Stop!' shouts Cillian.

After lunch in Los Andes, the cycling gets tougher and the road more inclined but spirits and energy are high. We're all focused as intensely as ever before. You reach a stage when the climb becomes enjoyable, when you find the right gear and a comfortable beat; climbing can be a better experience than downhill, a rhythmical Zen-like state where the mind becomes very clear and focused. You don't think or worry about how much farther uphill is left; in fact, you don't think about the road ahead at all.

We climb as far as Rio Blanco (1,450 metres). Successive punctures delay progress. Eventually we find Neil at a camping area called Guardia Vieja, a few kilometres farther on from the town and immediately adjacent to the Aconcagua River whose flow has become stronger the higher we climb. A horse canters back and forth in a field as we cross over to get to the river, strip off and wash. There are howls of pain as, one by one, we wade in. It's icy cold. Towards the river bank, up to my waist, where the water is not as fast, I stare back down the valley at today's progress and at Chile. Deep breaths in through my nose: the air up here is much thinner.

When the sun goes down, we light a barbeque and open a couple of bottles of the local red. Before now we had a rule not to drink as we cycled, unless we had a day off the following day, since we didn't want to lose focus; but things are more relaxed these days and sitting in the Andes with a glass of red is a great way of winding down.

'So the climb we've all been talking about continues tomorrow, boys,' says Kev.

'Argentina tomorrow,' Alan says.

'We certainly built it up, didn't we?' says John.

'There's no way it will be as tough as northern Peru; it just can't be,' I say.

'It's funny, when we were at home planning this, no one knew anything about Peru or about the Atacama. All the focus was on this climb,' Alan says.

The desert in Peru raised the bar in terms of pain and, judging from the climbing today, it would have to get ten times tougher tomorrow in order to compare with what it was like back then. The fantastic thing about putting your body through trials in places like Peru or the Atacama is the confidence it gives you. I look at the challenge of the Andes tomorrow and I fear nothing. The rest of the group is the same. The climb that some of us have been thinking about for years has been reduced to just another day on the road.

At the end of the two-day climb in the Andes, I feel satisfied to be crossing over to Argentina. The thought of the downhills to come eases the pain.

ARGENTINA

26 January 2009

Las Cuevas, Argentina

Number of days on
the road: 221

Number of kilometres completed: **17,452**

We take off, anticipating an increase in the intensity of the climbing and the gradient of the road. Both occur. The gradual climbing has come to an end. We turn a corner and see a series of thirty or forty hairpins stacked up, one on top of the other as far as the eye can see. This is the way to Argentina. The road looks like a giant ant farm. Trucks and cars crawl back and forward, up and down the road. A constant hissing of engine brakes fills the air. Myself and Rob, slightly ahead of the rest of the group, stop at the foot of the sequence to take a photo.

'Unbelievable, isn't it?,' says Rob.

I have to agree.

It's not always the natural wonders that are the most

impressive. Drivers in cars and trucks on the way down look at us, as if to say, 'Are you out of your minds?'

'I suppose there's no point in prolonging the inevitable, Benjamin. Let's keep up the momentum,' says Rob.

We get into the granny gear – slang for the easiest of all gears – and start out towards the first hairpin. The rest of the road is arrayed almost vertically above us like a stairs. Progress is slow but we make our way up, hairpin to hairpin, counting them off as we go. Each turn brings us significantly upwards and soon we peer down to where we stood looking up. There's a burn in my legs and I feel slightly light-headed. Halfway up, at a small lay-by, Rob and I take a break. A couple on a motorbike have also stopped.

'You're not far from the top,' says the man, getting off the bike and walking towards us.

They have come from San Rafael, a town 150 km south of Mendoza, he tells us.

His partner swings her legs from the bike and takes off her helmet, shaking out her long dark hair. Dressed in tight leather, she walks over.

'*Hola chicos,*' she says.

She lights up a cigarette and takes a long drag.

'*Hola,*' Rob and I say at the same time.

She's the first Argentinian woman we've met. We've been talking about Argentinian women for months. Mendoza has a good reputation.

'From Ireland,' I say to them both.

'Fantastic. Where are you going?' says the man, offering us cigarettes.

'Today, Las Cuevas. Eventually, Ushuaia,' I say.

'Wow! How much longer you cycle?'

'About five weeks, hopefully,' Rob says.

We shoot the breeze for another few minutes. They recommend bars and restaurants in Mendoza.

'*Loco* Irish men. But I love it!' says the woman, referring to our journey, as she walks back to the motorbike, getting ready to hit the road again.

'Be careful in Southern Argentina. Are you going through Patagonia?' asks the man.

'Patagonia . . . yes. No choice really. We'll nearly be home and finished by that stage,' I say.

'Well, good luck. If you cycle through Patagonia I have *mucho* respect for you,' he says.

'Tough down there?' asks Rob.

'You see with your own eyes!' says the man as he swings a leg back over his bike and fires up the engine.

'*Adios Irlandeses*,' calls out the woman as she clings tightly to her driver and the bike continues on its descent.

'I think I just fell in love,' Rob says.

With everyone back together again, the road flattens out and we arrive at Chilean customs, approximately 3,000 metres above sea level. The International Tunnel, which joins the two countries and where the road will begin to descend into Argentina, is just up ahead. Towering in the distance, standing out clearly from all other peaks, is Mount Aconcagua, covered in snow and perfectly visible. At 6,962 metres, Aconcagua, in Argentina, is the highest peak in South America, as well as in the southern and western hemispheres. (Mont Blanc in the Alps, for example, stands at 4,810 metres)

Our passports are stamped and, following behind the

support jeep, we cycle up to the tunnel. John and I roar 'Don't Cry for Me Argentina' as we cycle through and begin our descent. Our voices echo loudly against the tunnel walls. Moments after we exit, an enormous white and pale blue striped flag is flying at the side of the road. Even at this stage in the journey, there is a fantastic buzz in crossing a border; another country cycled through, another box ticked. After five minutes of downhill free-wheeling, we arrive at a large customs building and queue for permission to enter Argentina.

Las Cuevas, about 10 km from the border, is where we spend our first night in Argentina. The village is a base camp for mountaineers who are about to climb Aconcagua and men wearing thick mountain-climbing gear and carrying climbing poles wander about the village and sit outside the cafés. Travel agents sell mountain expeditions and a number of shops supply all the gear you need to put yourself on the peak. We find a campsite behind a hotel. It's full of hillwalkers and mountaineers on a budget, like ourselves.

My parents arrive in Mendoza tomorrow, so I'm going to take off early in the morning, a day ahead of the rest, and get down to meet them.

'See you in Mendoza,' I say to the lads before I turn in for the night.

27 January 2009

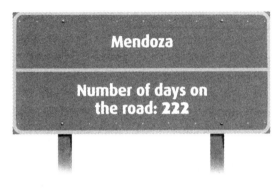

Mendoza

Number of days on the road: 222

Number of kilometres completed: **17,638**

I get up early, roll up my sleeping bag and climb out of the tent. Taking two panniers from the jeep, I pack enough clothes for the next couple of days, and attach the panniers to the bike. I also make sure I have two spare tubes, a pump and a multi-tool, in case anything goes wrong. Cycling solo presents far more problems.

As dawn breaks, I pedal out of the campsite and head towards Mendoza. The cycling is more gradual than the severe hairpins of yesterday evening. The road glides downwards and I'm not required to pedal at all, except to increase speed even further. I continue to follow the Mendoza River Valley and, after a fast 65 kilometres, arrive at the town of Uspallata. I stop to withdraw money from the ATM, eat and ring Dad.

'Where are you?' he says.

'About one hundred kilometres from Mendoza.'

'I suppose that means you won't be here until tomorrow?'

'I'll be there in four or five hours,' I tell him.

At Uspallata, there's a choice of roads to Mendoza: the 52 or the 13. I study the map and number 13, which follows the course of a river, looks more direct but I'm not sure which road has a better surface. I get on the bike and, taking a gamble, turn off for 13, the surface of which turns out to be fine. The road continues to drop. In my own mind I figure that, dropping down from the Andes, it will be all downhill but after I pass a lake, Laguna de Los Cangrejos, the road throws up a number of stiff climbs.

As I keep going, 60 kilometres from Mendoza, with much of the hard work for the day completed, I hear three loud snapping noises in a row: the unmistakable noise of the snapping of bicycle spokes. I jam on the front brakes. My left pannier has caught in the back wheel. I take off the back wheel and, being careful not to pierce the tube by forcing the spokes downward into the wheel, snap off the three offending spokes. The wheel will continue to work without the three spokes but, as time goes on, the imbalance will eventually cause it to collapse. I should just about make it into Mendoza before the wheel becomes useless.

Using a drawstring from trousers I packed in the pannier, I tie the pannier back, keeping it well away from the wheel. If any more spokes snap I'll be hitch-hiking. Looking back, monitoring the back wheel every few minutes, I continue down the road and eventually come to the main highway that leads to Mendoza.

The road becomes extremely busy. The hard shoulder is narrow, with a 6 inch drop to rough gravel on the other side.

It means a space of 3 feet exists on which to cycle between the heavy traffic and the gravel. Focused on arriving in one piece, I successfully keep the bike balanced on this narrow strip of tarmac and make it into the city centre where the ferocity of the traffic is less and the road more forgiving.

I find the page in my diary where I wrote down the address of the hotel: Plaza Independencia 627. I briefly look up and see that Plaza Independencia is right in front of me. I walk up the steps of the hotel and see Mum, Dad, with David and Hilary, Mum's brother and his wife, sitting outside, having a drink. Without them seeing me, I walk over and sit down beside them.

'Hello everyone,' I say.

Champagne slides down my throat like silk. I look at my family who have come all this way to meet me. Having battled hard on the road for seven months, this is a fantastic reward. The ups and downs of life on the road: one moment three spokes of your wheel snap, the next you're drinking champagne.

I check into a hotel a block down the road and we meet later for dinner at a steak restaurant called Don Pedros in Mendoza city centre. The steaks are the biggest I've ever seen. Argentina is famous for its beef as well as the size of the portions. We are invited into the kitchen to inspect the beef and the *parilla* (grill) on which they are cooked. My steak soon arrives at the table: the size of my forearm, it's served on a breadboard rather than a plate. After seven months spent eating tuna from tins, this is another challenge entirely.

The rest of the group arrive into Mendoza the following day and check into hostel accommodation. John's parents, Mary and Tony, have also flown out for a few days. Mark Gray, Alan's brother, has also arrived and will cycle with us for the next two weeks.

I head off with Mum, Dad, David and Hilary to a house on a vineyard near a town called San Carlos for a few days. I need some time away from the group. Living on top of one another every day can become intense and I reckon I'll be better equipped to take on the final weeks if I can switch off for a bit. Conversation about things other than maps, routes, borders and bikes is what I need. A comfortable bed, a bath and a lie-in are what I have been dreaming of. I'll rendezvous with the others back in Mendoza in a few days' time.

The time away is well spent. We go for a horse trek, taste wine and walk through the grounds of the vineyard. No thoughts of the end of the road, the condition of my bike or what lies ahead. My mind has become engrossed by this journey, by this road. Every day we think about nothing else: cycle, eat, camp, cycle, eat, camp. I wonder how long it will take to readjust to a more normal, less intense thought process when we return home. When the trip ends, what will each of us do to fill the gap that will be left?

Picnic Area,
(124 kilometres south east of Mendoza)

Number of days on
the road: 230–232

Number of kilometres completed: **17,982**

Having said our goodbyes, we cycle east out of Mendoza. I'm happy to get on the bike and get going again with the finishing line now very much in our sights. I'm aware of a slightly different mentality: for the first time ever, part of me is looking forward to the trip finishing. We are heading towards the Atlantic coastline. The plan is to cross over to Ruta 4, which runs south, parallel to the Atlantic Ocean, to Patagonia and to the end of Argentina. As we cycle out of Mendoza, it's warm and very dry. At an intersection, before we clear the city limits, the traffic lights go red and, while we wait to proceed, a fire hydrant bursts open and drenches us.

It's nice to start a new week on flat fast roads and, eventually, we find ourselves in the more familiar territory of open, sparsely populated countryside. The Andes cast a shadow on our backs as we leave them behind. Mark adds energy to the group and brings with him a fantastic no-nononsense attitude. He's a few years older than Alan and has been working as a carpenter in Ireland since he left school. I pair up with Mark for most of the day's cycling.

'I tell you what, Benny; you'll never have time off like this again. Enjoy the rest of this trip as much as you can. When you go home, it's a different story. Let's just say we're cycling home to reality!' says Mark, matter-of-factly.

'So, how bad is it at home?' I ask.

'Question is: how bad is it going to get? From working on sites for the past number of years, I've seen this coming. The game is over and the ball is burst.'

We turn off Ruta 7 and onto Ruta 153, a much quieter road, heading in a southerly direction. On either side of the road, there is dense, high growth. Visibility becomes poor compared to the open desert vistas that have become familiar. This is the farthest away from an ocean we have ever been and we find ourselves in the unusual surroundings of inland terrain. The temperature is higher than normal. There is no breeze to keep us cool. Sweating has intensified and greater amounts of water are being taken on.

Soon, things change again and there are no discernible features on the horizon, like a mountain, from which to gain a sense of progress; just flat plains of meadow. The road has no bends or turns, just continues for endless kilometres in a straight line, into the horizon.

We begin to see evidence of agriculture: fruit being picked from vast orchards and hundreds of cattle grazing on both sides of the road. At lunchtime, we stop at General Alvear hoping to find a restaurant or a supermarket to make sandwiches. Not a shop or business is open and there are no people on the streets.

'Someone tell them we were coming?' asks Brian.

'*Siesta*,' says Alan.

Unlike our experience in Chile, Argentina is very strict about its afternoon siesta. Businesses close, farm work stops and schools adjourn for approximately four hours. Everyone goes to sleep and towns grind to a halt.

Thankfully, there are a few spare loaves of bread and a number of tins of tuna in the jeep and we make do with what we have.

By the time we get back on the bikes and on the road again the town has come to life. It's 3.30 p.m. Shop shutters are lifted back up, children run and cycle back to school and the buzz and hum of voices and music fills the air.

We've now moved from Ruta 153 to 143. Punctures to Brian's and Mark's bikes delay progress. At 7.45 p.m., we arrive at our destination for the day, indicated by where Neil has pulled over in the support jeep. He has stopped on the verge of a large farm, between its gate and the road. A prickly, sharp shrub grows on the ground which we clear in order to lay the tents down. Neil bought steaks so we make a grill, barbeque the meat and bake potatoes by wrapping them in tinfoil and resting them against the hot coals.

'The Six Nations starts tomorrow. Ireland versus France,' Cillian says.

'Two chances of seeing that out here,' I say.

7 February 2009

Santa Isabel, La Pampa

Number of days on
the road: 233

Number of kilometres completed: **18,082**

At 7.30 a.m., we leave the camp and continue south, headed for the town of Santa Isabel. After a few hours, we take a break at a small roadside restaurant. Incredibly, at the back of the restaurant is a flat screen television showing the preview of the match between Ireland and France.

'I don't believe it! Come on Ireland!'

'All cycling is cancelled for the rest of the day,' Brian says.

We order some snacks and sit around, waiting for the match to start. The television is suddenly turned off. We all swivel around, jaws dropped, to discover an elderly lady grasping a remote control, standing behind our table.

'*Lo siendo, hombres. Siesta,*' she says.

She speaks a small amount of English.

'Excuse me: please allow us to stay here, there is a very

244

important match we would like to watch. Ireland are playing and we are Irish,' says Alan with all the charm he can muster.

'No. The shop must close. *Siesta. Muchas gracias,*' says the woman.

There is a collective sigh of disbelief. Not wasting time, we get straight back on the bikes and sprint 30 km to Santa Rosa to see if we can watch it there. When we arrive at the town, we split up, each of us scanning the gable ends of houses for satellite dishes. Brian spots one and we pull up to the house and knock on the door.

'*Hola Señor. Estaria bien si miramos un partido de rugby en su televisor?*' asks Brian

'Of course. I love rugby!' says Manuel.

He's a guy in his early thirties and looks like he may have even played rugby in the past. He seems delighted at the prospect of watching a match with us.

By the time we pile into Manuel's small living room the match has barely kicked off. He opens bottles of red wine and also offers us *maté*, the popular Argentinian herbal drink. *Maté* is a green substance made from the dried leaves of the yerba mate plant, boiled with water and drunk from a flask through a metal straw. *Maté* is a source of national pride. Locals carry around their *maté* kits in leather pouches, slung around their shoulders. Truckers drink it on long journeys; it's caffeinated and has an even stronger effect than coffee.

The match ends well and Ireland win. Our host Manuel stands at his door and waves us goodbye; another friend made on the road. We stay in the town and check into a local hotel. Restaurants don't open until 9 p.m.

12 February 2009

Number of kilometres completed: **18,275**

In the weeks ahead we must cycle through the desert of Patagonia. I've read Bruce Chatwin's *In Patagonia* and have a picture of the environment in my mind; a lawless and harsh cultural mishmash of a region. I suspect the place has changed since Chatwin's days down here but I am less convinced that it has changed in its physical harshness, as he describes in his book.

The landscape opens up as we arrive at the early stages of the transformation from arable countryside to barren wilderness. One of the best things about the bike is witnessing the gradual transition of countries. The change in the demeanour of the locals, the gradual increase in the power of the wind and the trailing off of areas of sizeable population indicate tougher times ahead.

On 10 February, a road sign indicates that we've entered

Patagonia officially. It excites me hugely as the mystery of the region has intrigued me for some time. I'd like to answer for myself the question of just how harsh the place is.

We take lunch at a YPF filling station and order rump steaks and chips. YPF, which stands for Yacimientos Petroliferos Fiscales, is an Argentinian oil company, partially owned by the state, and the most dominant along the road. The owners of the restaurant are interested in us. They ask us questions about the journey and, when we're finished eating, ask us to pose for photographs with them.

'You take care in Patagonia, boys!' says the waitress as we leave the restaurant.

The Patagonian wind unleashes itself after lunch; the animal is back. It roars from the south, more powerfully than in Peru or at any other time in the past. Staying on the bike is now a challenge. The wind doesn't drop or gust sporadically but hammers into us constantly, howling in our ears. We must shout at one another to be heard.

We take a turn-off and cycle east in the direction of Las Grutas, the first town we'll reach on the Atlantic coastline. We pass through a fruit-growing region; apples, pears and peaches abound. We're temporarily sheltered from the wind. The road is narrow and has no hard shoulder. Fruit trucks storm by regularly and make no attempt to slow down or give us a wide berth. On the outskirts of Villa Regina, Mark and I are out in front. There's a steep drop down from the edge of the road and, wary of the danger of trucks, we're forced to cycle on the extremity of the surface.

A truck barrels up behind us, making no attempt at all to provide space. He pulls directly alongside me. I look up and can see the driver perfectly in the cab. I make eye contact with him. I gesture to him to push over and give us some space. He does nothing and keeps his course. Furious, I look up, roar at him and give him the finger.

'Pull over!'

He swerves even closer, attempting to run me off the road. I'm forced to swing over the side of the precipice and tumble downwards. I hear the truck honking loudly as he continues on. I've fallen about 6 feet. I can see Mark, who has also been pitched over the side, picking himself up. I climb back up.

'Jesus Christ, that was close. He'd run straight over you and wouldn't even stop to look back,' says Mark.

Welcome to Patagonia.

I find the best thing is to cycle towards the middle of the road so that way the trucks are forced to slow down. There doesn't seem to be any safe way of doing things. At the end of the day, we arrive at yet another petrol station where, behind the shop, blocked from the road by a number of fuel containers, we set down on an open area of concrete. So that the owner can't object, we wait until the cover of darkness before we roll out the air mattresses and the sleeping bags. We don't bother with tents. Massive trucks, their headlights blazing, roll in and out throughout the night, the conversation of Argentinian truckers drifting in and out of our sleep. It's one of those nights where you just can't wait for the morning and the relative relief of being back on the road.

13–16 February 2009

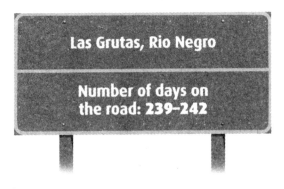

Las Grutas, Rio Negro

Number of days on
the road: 239–242

Number of kilometres completed: **18,781**

The wind blows straight from the south, hitting us dead on, unforgiving, never changing direction or giving us a break. Progress is energy sapping: we're making less than one third of our usual progress. After hours of heavy slogging, a vast blue ocean comes into view along the horizon. Cycling from the South Pacific to the Atlantic is something everyone will always remember. Though this particular achievement may become lost in the overall scheme of the trip, this is the type of challenge within a challenge that keeps interests high.

The Atlantic resort of Las Grutas is 1,070 km south of Buenos Aires. After the Pacific, the Atlantic is a refreshing change: darker, fresher and less refined. A rougher, less gentle coastline that feels more like home. As soon as we check into accommodation on the outskirts of town, myself and a few others grab our shorts and take a dip. The water is icy cold and a sharper reminder that the warm days of the Pacific, with its fragrances of fruit and herbs, are a thing of the past.

Rob and I arrange to meet Chris Wallace, a friend from Dublin who has flown out to join us. He got a bus down from Buenos Aires last night. Chris was set to start working as a business consultant in a few weeks but due to cutbacks the job offer was cancelled. This is the first living proof of the recession at home that we have encountered. With things the way they are, Chris reckoned, why not go cycling for a few weeks? He's learning Portuguese and plans to go to Brazil when this trip ends.

'Brazil is an emerging market, Benny. You got to follow the money, go where the next boom is,' he says.

'Brazil. What, forever?'

'We'll see; Ireland isn't a great place to be at the moment. No jobs. The game is up,' he says.

What a difference a year makes. When we left home things were still just about OK. Chris is still very much thinking of jobs, and the economy, and stuff we haven't been chatting about much at all. In fact, up to recently, it's been kind of hard to think about this trip ever ending.

'All this time on the bike and you mean to say you haven't even got one idea about what you're going to do?' Chris asks.

When people say they want to go away for an extended period of time and 'find themselves' or 'figure out what they want to do', I wonder what they expect. The countless hours I've spent on the bike haven't narrowed things down, as might be expected, or presented a clearer picture, but have opened things right up and, in the process, made the future less straightforward.

Las Grutas is one of our last major stop-offs before Ushuaia at the tip of Argentina. There are plenty of bars in the town and a nightclub overlooking the ocean that closes only when the sun rises. Our work attitude has certainly changed and our concentration is not what it was. We're staying out at night much later and drinking more than before. As a group, generally, we're not treating the road with the same respect we once did. Whereas before we were a disciplined, well oiled machine, now we are a disorganised, less focused group. A little part of all of us considers the trip to be over already. A part of my own mind is now at home, thinking about the future and the years ahead.

17–19 February 2009

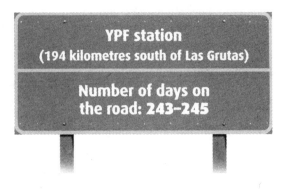

YPF station
(194 kilometres south of Las Grutas)

Number of days on
the road: 243–245

Number of kilometres completed: **19,169**

We take off again, this time with Chris joining the peloton. The wind makes a rare change of direction and blows from the west and northwest, which assists us in parts and makes progress faster. After 194 kilometres, at the turn-off point for Puerto Madryn, now in the province of Chubut, we pull into yet another YPF station.

Puerto Madryn was founded by Welsh immigrants in the mid-nineteenth century and some locals still speak Welsh. The town's flag is emblazoned with a dragon and, according to a man in the YPF filling-station, there's a thriving Welsh male voice choir.

When immigrants first arrived in desolate, windswept Patagonia they tried desperately to retain their national identities and Puerto Madryn is one such example. Similarly, there are towns and villages all over Patagonia constructed by Germans and Italians that still carry on the traditions of those first immigrants.

Following our standard procedure, we wait until the sun goes down before we set up camp between an unhitched trailer and the gable end of the YPF building; safe from the wind and out of sight. A steady stream of Brazilian and Argentinian registered trucks pull in to fill up throughout the night. The truckers look like tough, uncompromising men. They gather in groups at the petrol station and outside their trucks, smoking, chatting and laughing. Prostitutes, their gaudy bright clothes standing out in the barren landscape, move back and forth between the shop and the trucks.

The farther south we cycle, the harsher the countryside becomes, and the more unwelcoming-looking the people appear. It's not something we can immediately put our finger on, and maybe it's because Patagonia's reputation has preceded it, but there is a sense that things down here are unpredictable and dangerous. For one thing, there is no obvious law enforcement: Patagonia is so vast it cannot be monitored. This is where Butch Cassidy and the Sundance Kid came when the Wild West of America became too law-abiding.

The road runs straight: nothing to the west or east but barren grey plains. A basic wire fence runs parallel to the road and disappears into the horizon. The cycling is difficult and boring. There are no features on the landscape. We proceed slowly into the horizon, measuring our progress solely on experience and instinct.

'How far do you reckon we've done since lunch?' shouts John to those ahead of him.

'Not a clue; nothing is normal down here,' shouts back Alan.

We've been cycling for about a day and a half since Trelew, another Welsh settlement by origin and slightly bigger than Puerto Madryn. Herds of guanaco, animals like llamas but bigger, sprint across the road and into the distance. Where are they going? What's the rush? Large flightless birds called rheas run along beside us for several kilometres before disappearing under the fence and into the wilderness. We race against the rheas to try and break the monotony.

Stopping by the side of the road is almost as bad as being on the bike, as we struggle against the wind. With energy low, conversation is muted. We sit on the rocky, uneven surface, sipping water and commenting on the severity of the wind and on how difficult the cycling is. I think we were expecting an easy run to the end. This is frustrating for all of us at a time when we should be in high spirits, nearing the end and completing our goal.

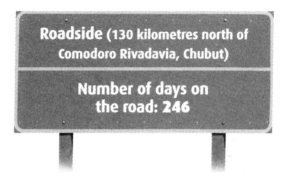

Roadside (130 kilometres north of Comodoro Rivadavia, Chubut)

Number of days on the road: 246

Number of kilometres completed: **19,239**

After about 50 km we stop for lunch. We're running low on food supplies, so Neil drives on ahead to find groceries. According to the map, there won't be any services for hundreds of kilometres, just one small village off the road, back towards the coast.

After another 80 km, we see the trailer in the distance. I'm delighted that another day's work is over. There's no sign of the jeep. Neil must have unhitched and driven down to the coast without the trailer. We pull up directly behind it and on closer inspection see that the lock has been removed. When we open the door it's immediately obvious that a number of items are missing. Either Neil has transferred them to the jeep or we've been robbed.

'What's he thinking? Why did he leave the trailer on the

side of the road unattended? Jesus Christ, lads, we're taking our eye off the ball, aren't we?' says Alan.

From what we can see, a lot of bike spares, tents, camp chairs and other stuff is missing.

Half an hour later, Neil comes back up the road.

'I'm sorry, lads. I left the trailer out so you'd know where to stop,' he says.

I know he thinks it's his fault but no one is pointing any fingers. This was a group mistake.

'Right, let's not waste any time,' Alan says. 'Anyone who had anything stolen, jump in the jeep and we'll go back up the road until we find a town with a police station. We have to report it. Not a chance we'll get the stuff back but for insurance we need to report it. Everyone else stay here; get the remaining tent up and eat something.'

I remain on the side of the road and prepare a meal. None of my gear was stolen. Later, nine of us pile into the one remaining tent for the night. We'll regroup in Comodoro Rivadavia tomorrow. It's the largest town of the Chubut region so we'll be able to replace stolen gear there. Let's reorganise in Comodoro.

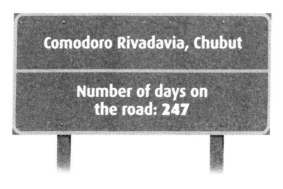

Comodoro Rivadavia, Chubut

Number of days on the road: 247

Number of kilometres completed: **19,687**

I wake up at midday. Thank God for the day off. We eventually got in last night to Comodoro Rivadavia, a large town on the Atlantic coast about 1,800 km south of Buenos Aires.

Kev and Brian reported the robbery in Trelew. The policeman making the report didn't speak English. We're pretty sure nothing further will happen.

All week, the wind gusting from the south has been in our faces, sometimes stopping us almost dead in our tracks. At the end of these tough weeks it's important to go out, have a good time and let off a bit of steam. That's what we did last night.

I pull myself out of bed, feel a slight hangover creeping up and walk a couple of blocks down to a Chinese buffet for lunch. The town is dirty with litter on the sides of the road.

On my way down, I pass a few groups of teenagers who are hanging around on street corners, smoking. It's Sunday morning so the town is quiet and most of the shops are closed. I'm just about to tuck into my noodles when Alan comes into the restaurant.

'Everything OK?' I ask

'We need to come up with €1,000 in the next half an hour,' he says.

'*What?*'

'One of the lads broke a door in the apartment last night and the owner of the place wants a grand for the damage.' Alan says, 'The police are going around the town arresting all of us as we speak.'

'Jesus Christ, is everyone OK?'

'Everyone's grand but we better get this money together quickly and get out of this town,' Alan says.

I leave the food on the table and we walk back towards the apartments. We rented two badly furnished, cheap apartments here last night. I saw the damaged chipboard door as I was leaving this morning, partially blown from its hinges and damaged at the top. Not €1,000 worth of damage. I'd say a hundred quid, tops.

Both of us withdraw the maximum amount of cash from the ATM and then continue quickly. I look over to the other side of the road and see John being loaded into a police car. The car then turns and drives towards us. It pulls up beside us and a policeman winds down the window and shouts at me and Alan to get in.

'Morning, lads,' says John, 'Would someone be so kind as to tell me what's going on?'

Five minutes later, in the police station, I look around

and see a lot of familiar faces; the rest of the group, thirteen in total, are in the holding cell already. No one is talking. Cordoned off by cardboard in a section of the cell is a woman who has been carrying out a protest for the past eleven years. Her son disappeared in custody here. There are pictures of him, with the caption 'missing', attached to the cardboard.

An hour passes. We try and ask one of the police officers what's going on but, despite our small amount of Spanish, we can't be understood. After another hour, an officer comes back in to us and tells us we're free to go. The police got it wrong. There's obviously been a mistake. *Adios amigos!*

But just hours later, we find ourselves on the street, surrounded by our bikes and other gear and equipment. Did that really happen? Did four policemen with guns really just demand 4,000 pesos and throw us on the street?

Still in shock, Neil fires up the jeep, we load the gear, get back on the bikes and cycle down into town. It's too late to camp. We haven't replaced the camping gear yet either. The Hotel del Mar is a tiny outfit owned by a Frenchman called Philippe Baguette and his Argentinian wife. He checks us in. We need a safe place to regroup and deal with everything.

Comodoro Rivadavia, Chubut

**Number of days on
the road: 249–250**

Number of kilometres completed: **19,687**

Philippe is a two-star Michelin chef and two times Miami Chef of the Year. When I arrive down for breakfast, he's sitting at the table, reading the newspaper. As I pour myself coffee and wander over to the sideboard buffet, Philippe turns to me.

'Is this you guys?'

'Excuse me?'

'Is this you guys who wreck the hotel?' asks Philippe, holding out the newspaper to show me the headline, which reads, in Spanish, 'Irish Tourists Wreck Hotel'.

'Hey, it's not what it looks like. We damaged a door and the cops took four thousand pesos from us.'

I can't believe that this has made the local newspaper. My heart jumps into my throat. I'm thinking about our sponsors at home. Our parents and our friends. I can't find the words to answer Philippe's questions.

'Things have been greatly exaggerated,' I say, worried that he won't allow us to continue to stay in this hotel.

'I know. I believe you,' says Philippe. 'The police here are horrible. This is not an unusual occurrence.'

I tell him that all we want is to keep our heads down and carry on down the road tomorrow.

'OK, but I help you. Four thousand pesos for this door is ridiculous!' Philippe says.

Neil has already heard that we made the headlines and soon everyone else finds out too. Sitting around the breakfast table we're thinking about the best way to deal with this. Cillian thinks this could be just the start of things.

'It's going to get home,' he says.

'All the way from here; from the middle of nowhere?' asks Kev.

'The internet, Kev. If an Irish journalist gets wind of this, they'd love to have a go at a group of college kids on a charity cycle, wouldn't they?' says Cillian.

'So what do we do?' asks Alan.

'We get our side of the story out first. We don't just hope this will go away. Let's post a blog on our website saying what actually happened,' I say.

I get my laptop out and, with the input of the rest of the lads, start writing a blog that will set the record straight and pre-emptively counter any articles that may be written at home. I write that things are going really well and that the trip is coming to an end. I say we went out for some drinks the other night and a bit of horseplay ended up with a damaged door. I continue to say that we were unlucky to

Luis Piedra Buena, Santa Cruz

Number of days on the road: 251–254

Number of kilometres completed: **20,232**

The story made it home to Ireland. An article appeared in *Metro* under the headline, 'Irish cyclists wreck hotel'. According to the article, we were drunk and threatening throughout our entire time in Comodoro Rivadavia. The landlord is quoted as saying that all he wants to do is run a quiet business and 'would we like it if he broke down our door?' He's then quoted as saying that people from the West have a sense of entitlement and treat places like Comodoro how they please. He makes no reference to taking €1,000 from a group of students in the presence of armed police.

'We're drawing a line under this, lads. No more talk about this. I'm not letting this ruin the end,' says Alan.

We cycle out of Chubut and into the province of Santa Cruz. Leaving Chubut behind provides a sense of relief. At least the bike allows you to move on from things. The mood in the group is quiet. We know what was reported in *Metro* was wrong but we also feel like we let our guard down, that we lost focus and concentration. We let someone take advantage of us and so we do feel we cannot avoid some of the blame.

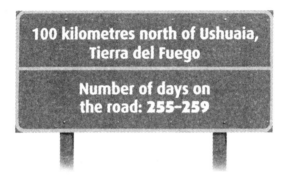

100 kilometres north of Ushuaia,
Tierra del Fuego

Number of days on
the road: **255–259**

Number of kilometres completed: **21,055**

We've been putting in tough kilometres for the past few days, hoping to put ourselves in reach of the end of the road by 6 March. We'd prefer a short, rather than a long, final day, so we can enjoy things. Today is Sunday. Nothing along the road is open; all shops and restaurants are closed. It's much colder now. We're wearing three or four layers of clothing and our hands are colder on the bikes. At night-time, the temperature plummets to only a couple of degrees above freezing. I need to wear a pair of jeans and several t-shirts before I get into my sleeping bag. Our camping gear is for summer and isn't designed for colder conditions.

After lunch, we cycle 40 km to where Neil and the support team have pulled into an access road. There appears to be plenty of space to set up. Jim and Neil have hot chocolates waiting. It means a lot after a cold, tough day. It's the small things that make the difference.

With the wind, the barrenness and now the cold, things are as miserable as they have been. You could so easily crack and get off the bike – give up – but it's too late in the day for that, and, anyway, we're still having a laugh and a joke about things. We haven't spent money on bike repairs for some time either, so many of the parts are on their last legs and the bikes significantly harder to cycle. I always thought these last days would be euphoric, easy and carried out with us all basking in sunshine. I don't think we expected to work so hard on the run in.

On 3 March, we have lunch 30 km north of the Strait of Magellan, the channel named after Ferdinand Magellan, the first person to navigate these waters successfully in 1591. Tierra del Fuego is actually an archipelago of islands, separated from mainland Argentina by the Strait. The territory of Tierra del Fuego is shared by Chile and Argentina but the Strait is largely the sovereign property of Chile. Until the Panama Canal, which we crossed at the end of last November, opened in 1914, the Strait of Magellan was the main shipping route from the Atlantic to the Pacific. Ships in the Strait, protected by mainland South America to the north and Tierra del Fuego to the south, can make the passage with relative ease. The Strait is approximately 570 kilometres long and just 2 kilometres wide at its narrowest point.

We soon arrive at the crossing point. A handful of cars and three trucks are already in a queue, waiting. The water is choppy and a cold wind blows into our faces. There is a fantastic sense of being at the cold, almost deserted, end of the world. You can imagine how exciting it must have been for Magellan's crew to find the crossing finally. The ferry *Patagonia* arrives and soon delivers us to Tierra del Fuego, the land of fire.

Tierra del Fuego's climate is less harsh than that of Patagonia but the roads are far worse. On 4 March, we cycle 122 km on unpaved gravel. The vibration from the surface through the bike is agony to my elbows, back and neck. We briefly cycle back into Chile, have our passports stamped again but are soon back in Argentina. No more border crossings until we're home in Ireland.

On 5 March, we enjoy tailwinds all morning. I had forgotten what it's like to have a prolonged period of progress without the wind constantly battering into us. We arrive at Rio Grande, the last major town before Ushuaia. Though it benefits far less from tourism and is less well known than Ushuaia, Rio Grande is the industrial hub of the Isla Grande del Tierra del Fuego, the biggest island of the Archipelago.

I pop into an internet café to check if anything else has been published in relation to Comodoro and see I've received an email from *The Irish Times*, wondering if I know anything about four Trinity graduates getting involved in an incident in a hotel in southern Argentina. Bad news spreads fast. I reply, giving our side of the story and referring to our blog. I let them know we're not making a big deal out of it. The email also informs me that the content of my latest column, which outlines the corruption we experienced at the hands of the Argentinian police, will have to be read first by lawyers. I'm assured it's a precautionary measure only.

The countryside has changed dramatically. No more windswept plains, just mountains covered in coniferous trees. Large lakes, sprinkled through the mountains, shine like mirrors. About 100 km north of Ushuaia, we rent a cabin on the shore of a lake for the night. It's hard to believe there's only one day left.

Day 259 It's our second last day and we can't help smiling at the thought that we're so close to the end of the longest road, *(l–r):* Chris Wallace, Ben and Rob Greene.

Ushuaia, Tierra del Fuego

Number of days on the road: 260

Number of kilometres completed: **21,155**

I often thought about how it might feel. In fact, I frequently wondered how it would feel. In essence, reaching today is what the whole trip has been about. People might say it was about the experience, the countries, the people, but ultimately it's about the end. Getting to the end – completion – is never far from the back of your mind. We set out nine months ago to cycle from Alaska to Argentina and now it's nearly done. Setting out this morning, I feel relieved and satisfied, not euphoric or triumphant.

When we get the bikes out of the holding shed, Alan says a few words.

'Lads, we've all been thinking a lot about today. But let's keep the heads, stay safe and we'll enjoy tonight. Last thing we want is a disaster today. Well done, lads. Now let's do this.'

We roar our approval and set out as a group for the last time. There's a sense of relief: all the pent-up frustration no longer needs to held back. No more wind, burst tubes or cold nights camping. No more nights in petrol stations or run-ins with crooked cops. But also, no more night skies packed full of stars, open roads or days and nights spent with people whom I'd go to war for.

About 30 km north of Ushuaia, we stop at a resort-style bar and restaurant and order 'Mountain Coffees', which are like Irish coffees but made with a local liquor.

'Remember the time in Mexico when we ran out of water and cycled on for 60 km without any?' says John.

'Not half as worrying as those borders in Central America,' says Brian.

And so it has already started, the recounting of stories and the retelling of memories. We sit around the table laughing and recalling happy and difficult times.

Brian and Alan carry the Irish flag into Ushuaia. We all cycle along, outwardly enjoying the moment but also thinking of everything else that has brought us to this point. I think about my family and the pride I hope this moment will give them. I think about how lucky I have been, to have been given this chance and to have completed it without suffering any harm. I consider how much of life is pot luck, just the luck-of-the-draw. Here I am at the end of the Pan-American Highway, living life to the full, while others haven't had such a big chance or aren't with us at all. I think for a moment of the short life of my late brother and reckon that this was something he would have loved to do.

Upon reaching Ushuaia, we realise that we must cycle another 25 km to the other side of the town to arrive legitimately at the end of the road, to where a plaque indicates you can't go any farther. The road runs through a national park and there's a guard at the entrance. He initially says it's too late for us to proceed, but then makes an exception when we tell him where we've come from.

Dusk is settling and we race quickly down the unpaved track. There's no conversation at this point, we're all dealing with the situation in our own way, wondering what it will feel like and getting ready to end abruptly what has been dominating our lives for the past nine months.

The plaque is a wooden structure measuring 10 feet by 6. Nothing like what we envisaged or dreamed of. We had expected more of a prize after nine month's effort. We open a bottle of champagne and hug each other.

We use the jeep to ferry people back to Ushuaia and, by chance, the last seven people who remain are the six people who started out in Alaska, and Rob, who did such a long stretch as well.

'Well that's it now. That's what we've been waiting all this time for,' says John.

'Home to Ireland. Well done, lads. Proud of all of you,' says Alan.

We finish off the last drops of champagne. Neil arrives back in the jeep and then we drive back up the road to Ushuaia.